first steps ®

Linking Assessment, Teaching and Learning

First Steps Second Edition was developed by STEPS Professional Development and Consulting (proudly owned by Edith Cowan University) on behalf of the Department of Education and Training (Western Australia).

It was written by:

Kevlynn Annandale

Ross Bindon

Kerry Handley

Annette Johnston

Lynn Lockett

Philippa Lynch

W9-CHC-279

Second Edition

Addressing Current Literacy Challenges

Authors' Acknowledgements

The *First Steps* Team from STEPS Professional Development gratefully acknowledges the contributions made by the following people.

Authors of Case Stories — Heather Griner, Bette Rees-Oakes, Jacqui O'Donnell, Margaret Poulgrain, Nigel Wardle.

To all the teachers and students who have been involved in trialling the materials and offering feedback whether as Critical Readers, Test Pilots, or Navigator Schools, we give our grateful thanks for you hard work.

The authors of *First Steps* Second Edition gratefully acknowledge and value the work of the authors of the original edition, developed by the Education Department of Western Australia, and the efforts of the many individuals who contributed to that resource.

Contents

CHAPTER 1
First Steps Second Edition

Why a Second Edition of *First Steps*?

First Steps Second Edition is the result of over a decade of reflection by teachers. Since 1990, teachers around the world have used the original *First Steps* materials to make practical connections between assessment, teaching and learning, and to cater for diverse needs within the classroom. They have strategically drawn upon the *First Steps* Developmental Continua and Resource Books to map the development of their students, and make informed decisions about appropriate teaching and learning experiences. The work of these many thousands of teachers, along with the valuable stories they have shared, has provided the impetus for ongoing, rigorous reflection and reorientation of the resource.

This second edition builds on the original *First Steps* resource by drawing upon contemporary research and developments in the field of literacy learning. It makes the links between assessment and teaching clearer and more explicit. This will help teachers to be more strategic about what to teach, how to teach it, when to teach it and, most importantly, why.

First Steps Second Edition has a strong focus on supporting teachers and schools as they embrace an outcomes-based approach to teaching. An outcomes-based approach in schools means a shift in emphasis from what is to be taught to what is actually learned by each student. The *First Steps* Second Edition will help teachers to maintain a focus on students and outcomes when the gravitational pull is sometimes towards covering curriculum content.

So What's Different?

Teachers familiar with *First Steps* will notice some significant changes to the resource.

• Strands

The second edition of *First Steps* is organised around four strands of literacy: Reading, Writing, Speaking and Listening, and Viewing. All strands are threaded with practical, accessible, classroom-tested teaching procedures and activities.

In response to the increasing impact of visual images on daily communication and the integration of print, images and symbols in multimedia texts, a Viewing strand has been added. Viewing is defined as the comprehension and composition of visual images, both moving and still, in a variety of media.

The Spelling strand in the original *First Steps* material has been incorporated into the Writing strand to emphasise the relationship between the two.

• *Organisation Within the Strands*

Within the resource each strand is further broken down into smaller categories, referred to throughout the resource as substrands. The strands and substrands reflect the change in how literacy is perceived and defined today. The types of literacy skills, knowledge and understandings needed by students to participate effectively in contemporary society have provided the basis for the overall organisational structure of the resource.

The substrands provide a lens through which student performance in all facets of literacy can be monitored and supported cohesively. The substrands, as defined later in this chapter, are:
• Use of Texts
• Contextual Understanding
• Conventions
• Processes and Strategies.

• The *Linking Assessment, Teaching and Learning* Book *(LATL)*

International feedback has contributed to a new, comprehensive, cornerstone book in the Second Edition of *First Steps: Linking Assessment, Teaching and Learning*. This book provides a means of reflecting on core understandings and beliefs about assessment, teaching and learning that are common to all strands of literacy.

• *The Maps of Development*

The *First Steps* Second Edition Maps of Development (formerly known as the *First Steps* Developmental Continua) are substantially more comprehensive.

The Maps of Development have been reconceptualised with an updated and revised set of indicators. The Maps now allow teachers to take into account their own practical research into particular individuals or groups of students, based on a factor of diversity and observed over time; for example, teachers can now allow for differences in linguistic background.

Suggested teaching emphases are clearly linked to phases of development and target specific areas of strength or need.

A revised and expanded range of teaching and learning experiences has been created at each phase of development. Combined, these improved features provide teachers with comprehensive support and clear pathways to make informed, strategic decisions about how best to support students' literacy development.

• *The Resource Books*

The Resource Books have been updated and expanded. Clear links can now be made between the Map of Development and the Resource Books through common organisational structures. New chapters dedicated to each substrand have been created. These provide concise theory and practical ideas for enhancing teaching and learning in each substrand.

• *CD-ROMs*

CD-ROMs have been added to the resource to help teachers access and manipulate formats suggested in the *Linking Assessment, Teaching and Learning* Book, the Maps of Development and the Resource Books.

Overview of *First Steps* Second Edition

The Nature of the Resource

The great irony of innovation in teaching is that the least tangible elements of the process are the most powerful. Too often it appears that a book or a collection of books is the key to positive change, where in fact the crucial factor is the teacher's engagement in sustained, practical, owned professional development. The subsequent coaching, feedback, discussion and reflection in a supportive setting are just as critical.

First Steps Second Edition is designed to complement carefully structured professional development processes that promote long-term commitment. Together the professional development and the books provide a strategic, whole-school approach to improving students' literacy outcomes. It is unlikely that *First Steps* Second Edition will reach its full potential as a teaching and learning resource without the combination of three important elements:
• quality professional development
• practical and comprehensive materials
• strategic planning for school implementation.

As a resource, *First Steps* Second Edition is only one part of an explicit and cohesive approach to improving literacy learning. It can be implemented in the company of other programs, and alongside a variety of resources and personal ideas. In doing so, schools and teachers need to be aware of the impact of competing priorities and how the different resources can work together to achieve common goals.

Given the breadth of literacy, schools and teachers may choose to implement only one strand or limited strands of the resource. Prioritisation makes sense and assists teachers to integrate new practices. Ownership and commitment to the implementation of *First Steps* is often engendered through the customisation of the professional development of a chosen strand. A selection of additional sessions, beyond the regular course, will be available to meet the needs of teachers in different schools and contexts. Attempting to implement parts of the resource smaller than a strand will generally result in piecemeal, disconnected outcomes.

The Structure of the Resource

First Steps Second Edition materials are made up of four interwoven strands of literacy: Reading, Writing, Speaking and Listening, and Viewing, which symbolise the interrelatedness of literacy learning. All strands are threaded with practical, accessible, classroom-tested teaching procedures and activities.

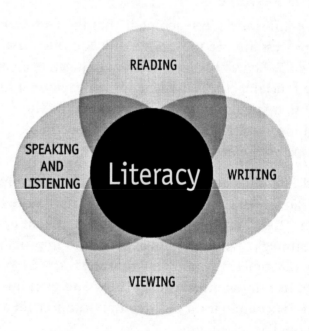

Figure 1.1: Strands of literacy

Within the resource each strand is further broken down into smaller categories, referred to throughout the resource as substrands.

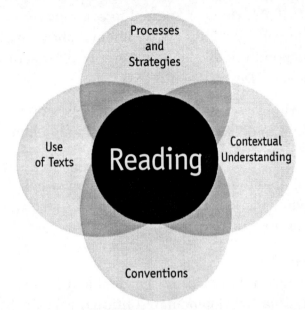

Figure 1.2: How substrands of literacy make up a strand, e.g. Reading

These strands and substrands reflect the change in how literacy is perceived and defined today. The types of literacy skills and understandings needed by students to participate effectively in contemporary society have provided the impetus for the overall organisational structure of the resource.

The *Linking Assessment, Teaching and Learning* Book

Research shows that teachers gradually integrate and adopt innovations based on their established understandings of what works best for students (Breen, 1997). This means that the teaching of literacy is underpinned by some personal, fundamental beliefs about what constitutes effective teaching. Consequently the core of the *First Steps* Second Edition is the *Linking Assessment, Teaching and Learning* Book (*LATL*) which:

- is an essential element of the professional development course for each strand
- provides an overview of the *First Steps* Second Edition
- enables teachers to reflect on how the beliefs underpinning the *First Steps* materials reconcile with their own personal and professional beliefs about teaching
- addresses aspects of assessment, teaching and learning that are generic and therefore applicable to all strands; e.g. **data collection**
- discusses management aspects such as classroom and school planning, creating a positive classroom environment and communicating with parents.

The Structure of the Strands

Each strand of *First Steps* Second Edition consists of two books, supported by a CD-ROM. One is dedicated to assessing the development of students and links developmental phases with appropriate instruction for individuals and groups of students. This book is the Map of Development.

The second book within each strand deals with the theoretical and practical background to different facets of that strand of literacy. This book is the Resource Book.

First Steps users will find that the Map of Development helps to assess and plan, while the Resource Book provides supporting detail about the nature of the strategies and activities.

The Maps of Development

The *First Steps* Second Edition Maps of Development (formerly known as the *First Steps* Developmental Continua) validate what teachers know about their students and are organised to help teachers link assessment to teaching. Although literacy in practice is an amalgam of the four strands of Reading, Writing, Speaking and Listening, and Viewing, individual Maps are necessary to represent the complexity of each strand.

Breaking each strand into substrands provides further opportunity for a more specialised analysis of the strands. These substrands allow teachers to focus on important aspects within each strand of literacy. The organisation of the Maps into the substrands provides a practical framework for looking at assessment, teaching and learning and reflects current beliefs about how literacy is defined.

The Maps of Development are based on long-term research and theory and suggest the broad phases of development through which a learner passes in becoming a competent user of that strand (Reading, Writing, Speaking and Listening, or Viewing). Each of the Maps contain behaviours, suggested teaching emphases and a range of teaching and learning experiences at each phase of development. Together these features help teachers make informed, strategic decisions about how to support students' literacy development.

• **Phases**

The Maps make explicit some of the indicators, or descriptors of behaviour, that help identify how students are comprehending and composing meaning. The indicators were drawn from research into the development of literacy in predominantly English-speaking students but many have been found to be applicable to students learning English as an additional language. They are essentially a 'what to look for', enabling teachers to be focused in their data collection, management and interpretation. It was found that indicators tend to cluster together; that is, if students exhibit one behaviour, they tend to exhibit several other related behaviours. Each cluster of indicators is called a 'phase'. This clustering of indicators into phases does not demonstrate that language develops in a linear sequence but does enable teachers to map student progress.

• Key Indicators

Key Indicators describe behaviours that are typical of a phase and are used collectively to identify a student's phase of development, so that links can be made to appropriate teaching and learning experiences. Additional indicators describe or illustrate development within a phase or movement toward the next phase. Individual students may exhibit a range of indicators from various phases at any one time. Students rarely progress in a neat and well-sequenced manner; instead they may remain in one phase for some length of time and move rapidly through other phases. Similarly they may show marked progress in one substrand but not in another. There are many factors that influence the rate and nature of a student's development, including sociocultural context, cognitive ability and the teaching and learning experiences offered to them.

The indicators within each Map of Development are organised under the following substrand headings:
– Use of Texts
– Contextual Understanding
– Conventions
– Processes and Strategies.

• Major Teaching Emphases

Major Teaching Emphases are also included at each phase of development. These are suggestions of appropriate teaching priorities for each phase and are organised under the headings:
– Environment and Attitude
– Use of Texts
– Contextual Understanding
– Conventions
– Processes and Strategies.

• Teaching and Learning Experiences

Teaching and Learning Experiences are provided in each phase.

These suggest different ways in which Major Teaching Emphases may be addressed and offer examples of activities designed to support students' development within the four substrand areas of literacy.

Figure 1.3 illustrates the relationships between Indicators, Major Teaching Emphases and Teaching and Learning Experiences documented in the Maps of Development. Once the indicators have been used to identify the student's phase of development, the combined selection of Major Teaching Emphases and Teaching and Learning Experiences, within the identified phase, will support further development.

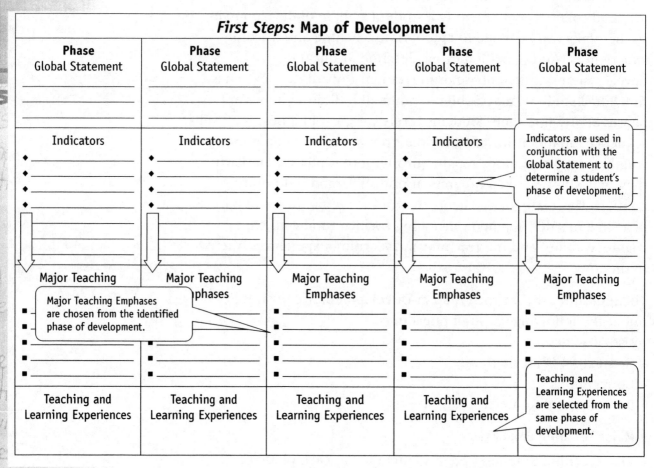

Figure 1.3: Relationships between Indicators, Major Teaching Emphases, and Teaching and Learning Experiences

The Resource Books

Each Resource Book explains the theory and critical features that underpin the strand within chapters dedicated to each substrand. The learning experiences of the Processes and Strategies substrand are also included in the Resource Books because these experiences can apply to students at all phases. The books also explore how to help students compose and comprehend spoken, written and visual texts for different purposes by providing an explanation of the structure and characteristics of a wide range of text forms.

CD-ROMs

Each strand includes a CD-ROM that provides teachers with access to any formats that have been provided in either the Map, Resource Book or *LATL*. These formats will always be identified with the CD icon. Parent Support Cards for each phase of development are also provided on the CD-ROM. Teachers are able to reproduce for classroom use, all formats provided on the CD-ROM.

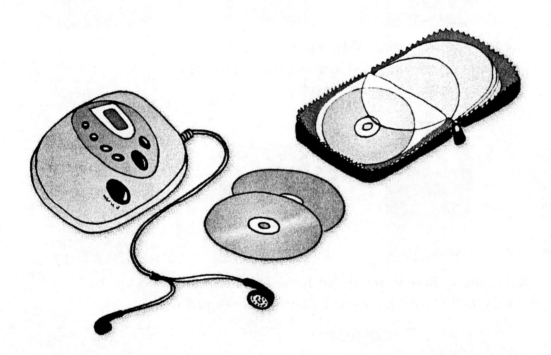

Overview of the First Steps Materials

Linking Assessment, Teaching and Learning Book

Linking Assessment, Teaching and Learning is a foundation text that supports successful assessment, teaching and learning.

First Steps Maps of Development

The *First Steps* Maps of Development provide phase-specific teaching and learning experiences that support students' development.

First Steps Resource Books

The Resource Books provide further information that supports teachers as they use the Maps of Development.

CD–ROMs

Reading   ***Writing***   ***Viewing***   ***Speaking and Listening***

The *First Steps* **CD-ROMs** include reproducible assessment and teaching formats, recording sheets and parent support cards.

Understanding the *First Steps* Second Edition Maps of Development

A number of essential understandings underpin the effective use of the *First Steps* Maps of Development. These understandings can be grouped under three headings:
- Exercising Professional Judgement
- Interpreting Indicators
- Considering Diversity.

Exercising Professional Judgement

Teachers using the *First Steps* Maps of Development can exercise professional judgement by considering the following understandings about the Maps.
- The Maps represent a progressive picture of what students do as a result of comprehensive and responsive literacy teaching.
- The Maps can be used by teachers in conjunction with school or state assessment and evaluation practices.
- The Maps provide a framework for, but do not replace, professional judgement in the areas of assessment, teaching and learning.
- The Maps provide a framework that supports professional judgement when the teacher is planning for whole-class, small-group and individual learning experiences.
- The Maps are designed to be used strategically; teachers decide how much data needs to be collected, about how many students, in how many strands and over what period of time.

Interpreting Indicators

- Indicators are recorded when they are displayed independently and observed on several occasions in different contexts, including other curriculum areas.
- Indicators are intended to be interpreted in the context of the global statement, the indicators from the surrounding phases and what the teacher knows about the student.
- Other indicators describe behaviours that provide further detail of the phase.
- Literacy behaviours demonstrated by students may be represented by a number of indicators in different substrands. For example, if a student uses a self-questioning strategy during reading to identify stereotypes in a text, an emphasis on the strategy used will see the indicator feature in the Processes and Strategies substrand; an emphasis on the student's knowledge of stereotypes, however, would see the indicator appear in the Contextual Understanding substrand.

- Ongoing collegial discussion about the interpretation of indicators is an essential part of the implementation of *First Steps* in a school.

Considering Diversity

- Social, cultural and linguistic factors have significant influence on student progress. The reason a student is or is not displaying an indicator is as important as the display of the indicator itself.
- Disabilities and varied learning styles may mean that some students need to display indicators with the aid of specialised communication equipment or means, such as braillers and specialised computer communication aids.
- *First Steps* Maps of Development can be annotated for individual students and groups of students by conducting systematic research. This can be done by noting the absence or addition of particular behaviours based on a factor of diversity observed over time. (See Chapter 4: *First Steps* and Diversity.)
- Students who have English as 'another language' may show indicators across a range of phases and may never fit neatly into one particular phase. This is true of all progress maps and assessment tools designed for broad student populations. For example, within an apparently homogeneous group of students who all share the same first language there will be significant variations in how literate each student is in that first language. The nature and timing of each one's previous experiences with English and a variety of social and cultural factors may affect an individual's development. It is critical that teachers employ professional judgement in assessing and evaluating the performance of students from diverse backgrounds.

The Maps of Development and Curriculum/Standards Frameworks

First Steps has been designed to support, not replace, a curriculum, a syllabus or a standardised assessment. *First Steps* has an emphasis on **how** students learn, unlike a curriculum or syllabus which has a strong focus on **what** students learn. *First Steps* has been designed primarily to help teachers make decisions about instruction, unlike a standardised assessment that has a focus on large-scale comparability of student populations. Attempts to 'equalise' or convert *First Steps* into a curriculum, syllabus or standardised assessment, or vice versa, are fraught with danger as each was written for a different purpose.

Most education systems have a curriculum or standards framework as a cornerstone of their endeavours. The framework normally sets out **what** all students should know, understand, be able to do and value as a result of the programs they undertake at school. Often this framework is accompanied by a standardised scale of assessment that measures whether these outcomes have been achieved, and the relative performance of subgroups within the student population. The primary purpose of an outcomes framework and standardised assessment is to describe and monitor performance so that it can be reported to stakeholders in the community.

In mapping terms, the education system is delineating destinations; that is, where the system wants students to be at a given point in their schooling.

Important destinations can also be found in the *First Steps* Maps of Development. However, a few significant differences between the two merit discussion. (See also Figure 1.4. on page 14)

- The Maps of Development allow teachers to find out **where** students are. The indicators are effectively towns on the way to the major destination. This fine-grained detail is valuable, as not all students will follow the same path to the destination. Some may move quickly while others may need some critical navigational advice.

- Unlike many curriculum and standards frameworks, the Maps of Development help teachers focus on **how** to support students in reaching their destination. The Major Teaching Emphases provided in the Maps of Development provide a strong suggestion of what is required to help students move from where they are to where they need to be. Without strategic, informed, responsive instruction the students may not be able to bridge the gap between their current performance (their current location) and the performance required by the education system (where they need to be). The Major Teaching Emphases within the Maps of Development enable teachers to make this critical link between assessment and teaching.

- The Maps of Development recognise that many factors affect students' learning. The phases of development cannot be equated with age or grade levels. Scope is provided for teachers to consider the influence of students' social and cultural backgrounds in determining where students are, and what is required to get them to their next important destination. Teachers are able to conduct action research into the impact of different factors on students' progress, and annotate the Map of Development to enhance its usefulness.

Relationship Between *First Steps* Maps of Development and Curriculum/Standards Frameworks

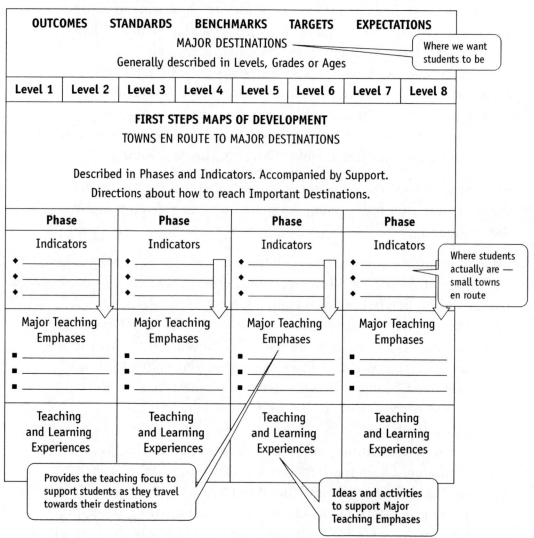

Figure 1.4

Defining the Substrands

Although they are strongly interrelated, any one of the four interwoven strands of literacy — Reading, Writing, Speaking and Listening, and Viewing — is a substantial area of focus in its own right. Traditionally curriculum developers have made the strands more manageable for teachers by breaking them down into component parts.

• Writing may have been divided into areas of ideas, structure, punctuation and grammar.

• Reading may have been considered in terms of comprehension and decoding.

While there is justification for many different ways of perceiving any area of learning, it is important that an organising framework is cohesive, that it amplifies rather than diminishes relationships between oral, written and visual language, and that it reflects literacy as a social and cultural practice.

On this basis each strand of literacy in the *First Steps* resource is organised into four significant areas referred to as substrands:

- **Use of Texts** — the comprehension and composition of a range of texts
- **Contextual Understanding** — how the context affects the interpretation and choice of language
- **Conventions** — knowledge of the structures and features of texts
- **Processes and Strategies** — application of knowledge and understandings to comprehend and compose texts.

The substrands provide a lens through which student performance in all facets of literacy can be monitored and supported cohesively.

Use of Texts

The 'Use of Texts' substrand focuses on the comprehension and composition of a range of texts. Texts are defined as any communication — spoken, written or visual — from which meaning is created.

There are many criteria used to sort the myriad of texts that students encounter. Within the strands regular references are made to written texts (Reading and Writing), spoken texts (Speaking and Listening), and visual texts (Viewing). Beyond the strand classification it is sometimes helpful to group texts as informational and literary. While it could be argued that every text is a creation and therefore no text can be considered purely factual, the distinction serves the purpose of categorising texts roughly according to purpose.

All methods of classification of texts overlap substantially. By returning to the primary purpose of a text to identify it, students assume a powerful position as composers and comprehenders. Identifying texts by their primary purpose enables students to take into account contextual understandings associated with the text.

The table (Figure 1.5 on page 16) categorises texts according to purpose. The broken lines indicate that modes, media, genres and formats are frequently interwoven in pursuit of that purpose.

An Overview of Texts

Tending towards literary text ◄─────────────────────────► Tending towards informational text

MODES	MEDIA	Entertain	Recount	Socialise	Inquire	Inform	Persuade	Explain	Instruct	FORMATS
WRITTEN	Printed	Narrative Poem Song lyric Fairytale Fable Myth	Biography Autobiography Diary Journal Retelling personal experience	Invitation Apology Message Note Personal correspondence	Survey Questionnaire	Report Label Menu Contents page Index Glossary	Exposition Menu Job application Editorial Headlines	Explanation Affidavit Memo Rules Policy Journal Timetable Complaint	Directions Timetable Recipe Manual Invoice List Experiment Summons	Magazine Letter Book Brochure Pamphlet Newspaper Chart Journal
	Electronic	Joke		Chat room						CD-ROM Text message Email Fax Card
SPOKEN	Live	Joke Story Song lyric	Conversation	Greeting Apology Telephone conversation	Interview	Oral report	Debate Discussion	Oral explanation	Oral directions	Performance Speech
	Electronic	Talking book Song lyric		Voicemail message			Talkback radio Song lyric			Audio cassette Radio Television CD-ROM Video
VISUAL	Live	Play Theatre								Clothing Tattoo Gesture
	Printed	Painting Photograph Cartoon	Picture book Photo				Logo Advertisement Catalogue	Timeline Graph Table Flowchart	Road sign	Button Flyer Poster Magazine
	Electronic	Television sitcom Film				Travel brochure	Advertisement	Documentary News report		CD-ROM Video cassette Web page

PURPOSES

Figure 1.5

Texts usually have a structure or pattern that results from the social and/or cultural context, and the purpose of the text. The dynamic and fluid nature of language means that the purposes and shapes of texts frequently merge and are subsumed into one another; e.g. a persuasive argument presented in a narrative form.

What students do with texts and how they are shaped to achieve these purposes are culturally specific. This is an important consideration in the assessment of a student's use of text. It is also important, however, to consider how students' spoken, read and viewed texts grow in sophistication over a period. The *First Steps* Maps of Development assist teachers in this monitoring process. This substrand illustrates how students can:
• expand the variety of texts they use
• enhance the control they exercise over the range of texts
• use and manipulate texts in complex ways.

This notion is perhaps most evident in writing. Consider the following two recount samples (Figures 1.6 and 1.7) that highlight differences in the complexity within the text and the students' control of the form.

Figure 1.6: Sample recount one

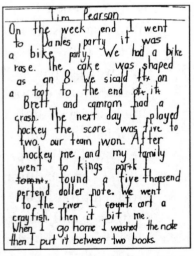

Figure 1.7: Sample recount two

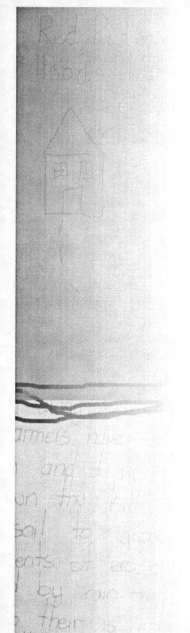

Contextual Understanding

The 'Contextual Understanding' substrand focuses on how the interpretation, choice of language and the shaping of a text vary according to the context in which it is used. From an early age children become aware that the language of the playground may not be as appropriate or effective in a more formal setting. Several factors influence the use of language:

- purpose of communication
- subject matter
- mode of communication (spoken, written, visual)
- roles of participants and relationships between them
- social situation.

Although some of these understandings of situational context are developed through imitation, observation and repetition, it is important that students are provided with opportunities to reflect on how language varies and needs to be amended according to purpose, subject, mode of communication and roles of communicators.

There are broader influences that impact on language use. All texts reflect to some extent the expectations and values of social and cultural groups. This understanding of sociocultural context involves knowing that:

- the way people use language both reflects and shapes their sociocultural outlook — the beliefs, values and assumptions of their sociocultural group, especially with regard to gender, ethnicity and status
- texts will be interpreted differently by different people according to their sociocultural background — awareness of the influence of sociocultural factors on composing and comprehending is pivotal
- language and culture are strongly related
- language is crafted, communicated and manipulated to influence others, often to maintain or challenge existing power relationships between groups such as employers and employees, businesses and consumers, or governments and citizens
- there are many varieties of English used around the world that reflect and shape sociocultural attitudes and assumptions, including the Standard English that is generally used in formal communication, education and some professional settings.

Conventions

The 'Conventions' substrand focuses on the knowledge of the structures and features of a variety of texts. Different sociocultural groups may adopt different legitimate conventions in their use of language. It is imperative that students become aware of the language structures and features that are typical of Standard English so that they are able to have access and influence in formal settings. Effective language users are able to act on their awareness of contextual understandings to make choices about the mode of communication, the type of text, the grammatical structures, the presentation style and the words that are most appropriate and effective in a particular setting. They are able to talk about the choices they have made and the language structures and features they can recognise in their daily encounters with authentic language. For example, students preparing a recount of a school event for a local newspaper may conclude (after reading several newspaper articles) that they need to use a particular text structure and its grammatical conventions to meet the expectations of the paper's readers.

Examples of Conventions Associated with Spoken, Written and Visual Texts

- Patterns of text structure and organisation (selection and sequence according to purpose and text type)
- Textual cohesion (pronoun reference, conjunction)
- Grammar (tense, agreement of subject and verb, passive or active voice)
- Vocabulary and tone (specialised vocabulary, colloquial/formal, connotation/nuance)
- Stylistic features (figurative/rhetorical, analogies, irony, alliteration)

Examples of Conventions Specific to Spoken Texts

- Intonation, rhythm, pace, pitch, volume, pauses
- Pronunciation and enunciation
- Nonverbal language (facial, body movement, proximity, gesture)

Examples of Conventions Specific to Written Texts

- Print elements (letter, word, spacing)
- Paragraphing and punctuation
- Spelling
- Layout and presentation
- Referencing style

Examples of Conventions Specific to Visual Texts

- Conventions of the technical code (lighting, camera angles, special effects)

- Conventions of written and audio codes (theme music, commentary)
- Conventions of the symbolic code (colour, clothing, setting)

Processes and Strategies

The 'Processes and Strategies' substrand focuses on the application of knowledge and understandings to comprehend and compose texts. Whether students are comprehending or composing they are acting upon what they know about how texts work. Some strategies are employed intuitively, particularly in familiar contexts with familiar people. However, unfamiliar contexts and participants, more complex texts and sophisticated purposes require the deliberate selection and manipulation of processes and strategies from a versatile repertoire.

Examples of Processes and Strategies Used by Students When Reading

- Skimming and scanning to select a text or find specific information
- Connecting prior knowledge to information in the text
- Breaking words into parts such as phonemes, attaching sounds, and combining the parts
- Predicting storyline from the title, cover or pictures

Examples of Processes and Strategies Used by Students When Writing

- Planning, drafting, revising, editing and proofreading
- Researching and note-making
- Recalling, inventing and consulting when spelling
- Copying words from the environment

Examples of Processes and Strategies Used by Students When Speaking and Listening

- Listening for pauses, changes in tone and key words to monitor spoken texts
- Staying on the topic and making relevant contributions to conversations and discussions
- Making notes, rehearsing and refining formal spoken presentations
- Questioning to elicit information

Examples of Processes and Strategies Used by Students When Viewing

- Drawing on prior knowledge and experience to predict text structure
- Using knowledge of conventions associated with viewed texts to interpret meaning; e.g. colour, music, symbolism, camera angles

- Self-questioning to clarify content
- Making connections to own experiences

The Assessment, Teaching and Learning Cycle

Once a strand has been selected as an area of need, the *LATL* Book can be used in conjunction with the Map of Development and the Resource Book. Effective teachers create unique pathways as they make decisions about assessment, teaching and learning. These pathways are rarely linear and in a single direction, but they do appear to incorporate at least four essential elements. In a cyclic manner, consciously or subconsciously, teachers tend to:

- evaluate student needs
- identify resources and plan
- select teaching and learning experiences
- monitor student progress and teacher effectiveness.

Revisiting and reflecting occur frequently and often act as a directional force in the process.

The *First Steps* resource has been designed to aid the assessment, teaching and learning process. The Assessment, Teaching and Learning Cycle (Figure 1.8 on page 22) illustrates how teachers can navigate *First Steps* Second Edition by selecting and using parts of the resource that assist their natural cycle of teaching and reflection. Although most teachers will move in a clockwise direction, from 'Evaluating Student Needs', the personal pattern of movement is an inward and outward one (in star or flower-petal fashion). As teachers become familiar with placing students on the Maps of Development and with the different parts of the resource, the balance between what is effectively in-head knowledge and what needs to be referred to in the text will shift. Resources other than *First Steps* are used to supplement the cycle. The options explored on each pathway of the Assessment, Teaching and Learning Cycle are rarely the same, as teachers continually improve the integrity, validity and efficiency of what they do.

Assessment, Teaching and Learning Cycle

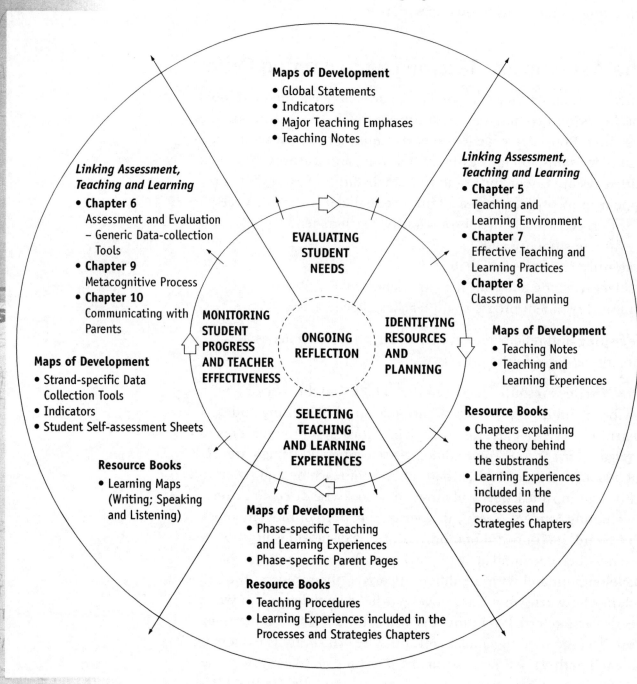

Maps of Development
- Global Statements
- Indicators
- Major Teaching Emphases
- Teaching Notes

Linking Assessment, Teaching and Learning
- **Chapter 6**
  Assessment and Evaluation – Generic Data-collection Tools
- **Chapter 9**
  Metacognitive Process
- **Chapter 10**
  Communicating with Parents

Maps of Development
- Strand-specific Data Collection Tools
- Indicators
- Student Self-assessment Sheets

Resource Books
- Learning Maps (Writing; Speaking and Listening)

Linking Assessment, Teaching and Learning
- **Chapter 5**
  Teaching and Learning Environment
- **Chapter 7**
  Effective Teaching and Learning Practices
- **Chapter 8**
  Classroom Planning

Maps of Development
- Teaching Notes
- Teaching and Learning Experiences

Resource Books
- Chapters explaining the theory behind the substrands
- Learning Experiences included in the Processes and Strategies Chapters

Maps of Development
- Phase-specific Teaching and Learning Experiences
- Phase-specific Parent Pages

Resource Books
- Teaching Procedures
- Learning Experiences included in the Processes and Strategies Chapters

EVALUATING STUDENT NEEDS

IDENTIFYING RESOURCES AND PLANNING

ONGOING REFLECTION

MONITORING STUDENT PROGRESS AND TEACHER EFFECTIVENESS

SELECTING TEACHING AND LEARNING EXPERIENCES

Figure 1.8

CHAPTER 2

Planning for the Successful Implementation of *First Steps*

The Successful Implementation of Change

As *First Steps* continues to be implemented in thousands of schools throughout the world, several factors that most often characterise successful implementation have been identified. Leaders in the field of educational change: Bruce Joyce and Beverly Showers, Barrie Bennett, Susan Loucks-Horsley, Dennis Sparks and Michael Fullan, have influenced the creation of the framework recommended by *First Steps* for successful implementation. This implementation framework includes a number of factors being considered at both the classroom and school level:

- High-quality Professional Development
- Principal as Learner and Leader
- Ongoing Support for Teachers
- Whole-school Implementation
- Providing Time
- Maintaining Continuity Through Planning
- Reflecting and Celebrating
- Developing and Articulating a Vision
- Monitoring and Evaluating the Outcomes
- Involving Parents.

These particular characteristics underlie any successful change effort. They are not ordered, but the absence of any one of them has the power to dilute the impact *First Steps* may have on improving student outcomes.

High-quality Professional Development

Classroom teachers use *First Steps* materials most effectively when the texts are coupled with high-quality professional development. In *First Steps*, professional learning is viewed as a recursive process of attending courses, applying new learning, exchanging ideas, reflecting on practice and collaborating within a school community. The *First Steps* texts provide an excellent vehicle for this process and have not been written to 'stand alone'.

Schools successfully implementing *First Steps* commit to one strand of *First Steps* professional development at a time (Reading, Writing, Speaking and Listening, or Viewing). It is critical that professional development courses be followed up with ongoing sessions within each school. These follow-up sessions may take the form of study-group meetings, year-level meetings, collaborative planning sessions, further workshops, modelled lessons and peer coaching or attendance at related courses or conferences.

Staff development should not be perceived as something we do unto the weaker teacher or reserve for inexperienced staff members. All staff members, including principals, consultants, and teacher mentors, should be able to announce, 'This is my year to study …'

There needs to be a genuine feeling that no one has arrived. Everyone needs to be swept up by the deeply ingrained value placed on adult learning.

Shelley Harwayne
Stenhouse Newslinks: Professional Development Corner
(September 2002)

Principal as Learner and Leader

Leadership is critical to a school's successful implementation of any professional development program. School leaders play a vital role in creating an environment that is conducive to the implementation and institutionalisation of any innovation. School leaders can create this type of supportive environment in a number of ways.

- Clarify expectations
- Participate in professional development sessions
- Provide encouragement
- Organise resources such as money, materials and time
- Limit distractions
- Facilitate support for teachers
- Promote an ethos of a community of continuing learners within a school
- Participate in the school community as a partner/mentor to teachers.

Teachers need to know from the outset that *First Steps*, as a professional resource, is supported and valued by the principal and other school leaders. Visibility, presence and participation of school leaders in *First Steps* professional development sessions communicate powerful messages about the importance of the resource for students, teachers and the school community. Most importantly, participation in professional development will provide principals with the necessary understandings and processes to effectively support the implementation of *First Steps* across the school.

> *The Principal Principle: it means that the further the principal is from the innovation, the faster he/she will expect you to implement it and with less support and resources than you need.*
>
> **Barrie Bennett, 1995**
> PETA — Primary English Teachers Association (PEN 102)

Ongoing Support for Teachers

Research supports the notion that 'one-day wonders' or isolated training sessions are unlikely to result in significant changes in the classroom setting (Fullan, 1991; Joyce and Showers, 1995). Optimal professional development for teachers consists of high-quality courses presented over time, combined with processes that provide ongoing support to translate the new learning into classroom practice. Sustained practice is necessary to incorporate any new learning into regular classroom procedures. Ongoing feedback and support are crucial in the implementation of *First Steps*.

First Steps is based on the belief that effective implementation requires multiple opportunities to learn, experiment, observe, reflect, discuss, refine and adapt the new understandings, skills and processes presented during the professional development courses. It is essential that schools implementing *First Steps* plan for the time and structures that will allow teachers to collaborate with others during implementation.

> *… a large dramatic increase in transfer of training occurs when in-class coaching is added to an initial training experience …*
>
> **Bruce Joyce and Beverly Showers, 1995**
> *Student Achievement Through Staff Development, page 112*

Whole-school Implementation

School-wide improvement efforts that focus on shared team goals help create a collective commitment to student learning. Linking the initiative to current school-improvement goals can stimulate a shared commitment to new professional development initiatives. Research highlights that schools and staff improve by promoting both individual and organisational growth and by working together. For effective change to occur, a new professional development initiative should belong to a whole staff. A new initiative may often begin with one person or a selected few within a school, but ultimately should result in a whole-school commitment. Implementation at a whole-school level is an important factor to consider when using *First Steps*.

... whole-school and whole-district programs often achieve higher rates of transfer than do programs that involve small groups of volunteer teachers from schools.

Bruce Joyce and Beverly Showers, 1995
Student Achievement Through Staff Development, page 13

Providing Time

Learning takes time. Finding time to attend professional development courses, to integrate new ideas into classroom practice, to collaborate about new ideas and to work as a whole school to create ongoing implementation plans is a constant challenge faced by all schools implementing any new initiative. Those schools that recognise learning as a process and not merely as an event provide opportunities for continuous learning. These schools also create realistic implementation timelines that acknowledge existing commitments and priorities within the school.

First Steps professional development courses are most effective when they are conducted over time, providing participants with the benefits of spaced learning and thus avoiding information overload. These courses can then be interspersed with ongoing support and reflection sessions.

Nothing is gained by having time-efficient staff development efforts that produce no significant teacher learning.

Loucks-Horsley et al., 1987
Cathy Miles Grant Web Page

Teachers often cite the provision of time to work with others as the most valuable form of ongoing support. Schools that have worked hard to create time for teachers to reflect and work with others as they implement *First Steps* have demonstrated a commitment to the importance of collaborative learning. Many of these schools re-examined existing structures and schedules to create common times for teachers to meet together.

Following is a compilation of innovative ways in which schools have created TIME for ongoing learning.

- Providing common planning or preparation time for same-year-level teachers
- Hiring roving relief/substitute teachers to release teachers from classrooms
- Allocating time at regular staff meetings for *First Steps* discussions
- Providing breakfast for meetings before school — 'Breakfast Club'
- Releasing teachers from classrooms — principal providing relief
- Reviewing school start and finish times to create a monthly 'early release' day
- Making use of school assemblies or other school-wide events to release pairs or small groups of teachers.

Maintaining Continuity Through Planning

Any new initiative will be more successful when teams of people work together to create continuous plans of implementation. Ongoing whole-school planning for implementation is essential and can often be identified as critical to the success of *First Steps* in schools.

Regular participative decision-making sessions involving all staff allow for the development of implementation plans that can then provide the momentum for the transference of *First Steps* materials into the classroom. Plans created by staff are most effective when they:

- are short term (four to six weeks) and flexible
- provide a framework for reflection and evaluation
- support the needs of teachers
- document a minimum requirement for implementation
- promote progress.

A big vision with small building blocks can create consensus and progress.
Michael Fullan, 1993
Change Forces, page 62

Figure 2.1 on page 28 provides an example of an implementation plan created over time by a school staff.

Whole-school Planning for Implementation			
Date	What	By When	Resources
20 Aug	Predict whole class using Global Statement Place 3 students on Writing Map of Development (WMD) Indicators Trial Modelled Writing 3 x 4	17 Sep	Class Profile sheets Individual Profile sheets Flip charts *First Steps* video
17 Sep	Attend Data Collection Methods Workshop Trial 4 different data-collection methods, presented during training (LATL and WMD books) Year-level meeting for Key Indicator Review Session Introduce DEAW (Drop Everything and Write)	24 Sep 10 Oct	*Linking Assessment, Teaching and Learning* (LATL) and WMD books Relief teacher for Year-level meetings
13 Oct	Continue to trial data-collection methods Include Look What I Can Do sheets Place 3 students on WMD using Key Indicators	10 Nov	Look What I Can Do sheets Individual Profile sheets
10 Nov	Place 5 students on WMD using Key Indicators Select Major Teaching Emphases (MTEs) related to phases in class Select activities from WMD to support MTEs	1 Dec Bring MTE/ Activities to share	Individual Profile sheets WMD and Writing Resource Book (WRB)

Sample Only

Figure 2.1: Sample of whole-school plan for implementation of *First Steps*

Reflecting and Celebrating

In schools introducing *First Steps* it is important to have a climate that encourages ongoing reflection and self-evaluation by teachers. The process of whole-school planning provides a perfect forum for groups of teachers to reflect on successes, ponder questions, and discuss issues about implementation. Reflective discussions about agreed goals, student outcomes and teaching strategies can drive the development of new plans and allow staff to continue to move the *First Steps* implementation process forward at an appropriate pace. Improvements in student outcomes that are shared and celebrated by school communities create a sense of achievement that can drive further implementation. Principals can motivate the staff to maintain efforts by recognising and acknowledging group and individual contributions.

Developing and Articulating a Vision

It is important for schools to have a mental image or clear vision of what the successful implementation of *First Steps* might look like in the long term. What might students, individual teachers, teachers as a whole team and parents be doing as a result of introducing this resource? Creating this shared vision ensures a common set of expectations and goals for everyone to work towards. The following table (Figure 2.2) reflects the practices that would be evident in a school successfully using *First Steps*. The list can be used as a framework for schools to create their long-term goals and to reflect on their implementation achievements.

Goals and Expectations for the Implementation of *First Steps*	
Students	• are actively involved in meaningful and developmentally appropriate learning experiences • are metacognitive about their learning and set goals for future achievement • display measurable and observable progress • select and apply their literacy skills and understandings to a variety of contexts.
Individual Teachers	• use assessment practices that are valid, educative, explicit, fair and comprehensive • critically analyse the information collected to make judgements about student progress • use Major Teaching Emphases and Teaching Notes to make strategic decisions to target student needs • select from a wide range of teaching and learning experiences to target student needs • understand that *First Steps* in practice will vary from context to context, but will be recognisable by the essential element of linking assessment to teaching • continually reflect and refine their teaching practice to achieve student outcomes.
Whole Schools	• strategically plan to support the implementation of *First Steps*, encouraging whole-school involvement in consensus-driven, ongoing professional development • are aware of, and value, the elements of time, space and support in the *First Steps* implementation process • recognise the principal's role as key educational leader • use ongoing processes for collaboratively creating short- and long-term plans for the implementation of *First Steps*.
Parents/ Caregivers	• are informed about their child's literacy development through the sharing of information including strategies to support their child's literacy development in the home • are invited to provide information about their child's literacy development • are encouraged to be actively involved in the school environment.

Figure 2.2: Created by Dale Elementary School, 2001

Monitoring and Evaluating the Outcomes

Monitoring and checking progress throughout the implementation process is a key element in schools that are using *First Steps*. Staff should be involved in setting standards for assessing the effect of *First Steps*. Principals then play a major role in gathering evidence about the learning, application of learning and impact on student outcomes. Figure 2.3: Kirkpatrick's Model of Evaluation (1996) can easily be applied to schools and provides principals with a framework for evaluating the different outcomes of implementing *First Steps*.

Kirkpatrick's Model of Evaluation
Level 1: Participants' Reactions
Level 2: Participants' Learning
Level 3: Application to 'On-the-job'
Level 4: Impact on Student Outcomes

Figure 2.3

Information at the different levels can generally be gathered through a range of data-collection tools.

Involving Parents

Schools that are successfully using *First Steps* have made a conscious commitment to involve and inform parents and caregivers before and during the process of implementing the new resource. From the outset, parents and caregivers have been informed about the upcoming professional development courses, the goals and the expected impact on their child's or children's education. After teachers have attended professional development courses, many schools have organised information sessions for parents and caregivers to provide them with an overview of the *First Steps* resource. Teachers have then provided parents with ongoing information designed to help support literacy development in the home.

Teachers using the *First Steps* resource recognise that schools build on the successful learning that is provided in the home by parents. *First Steps* is based on the belief that parents and teachers working together in partnership will help children achieve success.

CHAPTER 3
Understanding *First Steps* Beliefs

The Art of Teaching Literacy

Effective teaching is a complex, personal act that requires constant reflection, collaboration and support. Of the many decisions teachers make each day, few are formulaic. What's best for one student may not be best for others. It may not be what the curriculum suggests, or what can be achieved with limited time and resources. Simple answers in the form of a single book, professional development course or sweeping new initiative are generally cruel illusions. Effective teaching is challenging.

Teaching literacy effectively is even more challenging. It's not like teaching someone to change a car tyre. Tyres the world over are round and made of rubber, whereas being literate can look different depending on where you are, whom you're communicating with, what you're trying to achieve and whether you're trying to make meaning through print, oral language, visual imagery or a combination of these resources. That's one of the reasons why many educators are talking about many different literacies, rather than a single set of cognitive skills that enable a person to be universally literate. The spoken language of the corporate world might be useful in the boardroom but has limited impact in the street. What counts as literacy varies from context to context and who decides what counts as literacy also changes. Literacies are neither neutral nor static.

New technology will lead to improved tyres in the future, as it has done in the past, but the tyre will remain generally round and made of rubber. In contrast, the rapid, relentless development of information communication technology is making significant differences in the nature of literacies. Mobile phones are dragging once-private phone conversations into public arenas. Emails are being used to distribute jokes and stories once shared in a social chat. Consumers are being ambushed by information carefully orchestrated across print and television, online and live-performance media. As social practice, literacies reflect the advances in information communication technology in profound ways.

Finally, changing a tyre is a narrow, procedural act that relies on some fundamental understandings about simple mechanics. Reading, writing, speaking, listening and viewing, on the other hand, are practices that often rely on social and cultural expectations. They are not simply feats of the mind or natural ways of doing things. They occur to achieve particular purposes and therefore make no sense when they are divorced from a meaningful context.

Introducing students to the ways in which language is used to get things done is a subtle and changing art that varies according to a student's social and cultural understandings. Teachers confronted with these understandings recognise the similarities and differences between the literacy being taught in schools and the literacies that students use at home and in the community.

Whose Literacy?

Learners are different. Dale, Khaleda and Alejandra live in settings that are geographically, socially and culturally worlds apart, although they could just as easily be seated next to each other in one classroom. They wake up each morning to different family arrangements and speak different languages, dialects and forms of English. They view the day's events through a unique personal lens and have different social and cultural ways of doing things. Dale nods his head to his brother to indicate that it is time to head off to school. Khaleda engages in a long and practised routine of kisses, 'high-fives' and personalised farewells. Alejandra sends off a brief email with digital photos to her dad before racing out the door. Yet for all their differences, Dale, Khaleda and Alejandra share a basic human desire to communicate by making meaning.

Literacy for each learner means something slightly different in action, but has a common core.

- There are common understandings about who will understand these morning routines, gestures and messages and who will not.
- There are common and changing understandings about whether these messages are most meaningful:
  - face to face (supported by nonverbal cues)
  - on paper (in permanent visual symbols)
  - through an electronic medium (appearing on a screen).
- There are common understandings developing about the language forms that are used to get things done within and beyond the community.

Varied purposes, participants, contexts and subject matter mean that shared understandings about literacy may look different in action. Both within classrooms and across a school, teachers face the challenge of acknowledging and building upon the diversity students bring to their learning.

Dale could be taught the procedure of composing and sending an email, but it would make little sense to him without an authentic purpose and audience. Alejandra could be taught the meaning of the nod, the eye contact and the body language associated with Dale's departure, but its use would probably leave her siblings and peers amused and confused. Khaleda could probably explain her affectionate morning rituals, but only by elaborating on her family structure and relationships. What these frequent, tailored acts of communication have in common is that they find meaning in social and cultural settings.

Students from different cultural backgrounds learn in one classroom.

Teachers also come from a range of social and cultural backgrounds. They are faced with the challenge of helping students develop a versatile, shared core of understandings that will provide the foundation for the mastery of new and unfamiliar types of literacies. This means helping students make connections between what they know and what they need to know to live, work and socialise in different settings with different cultural groups at different times.

The Reflective Teacher

First Steps is underpinned by the belief that constant reflection and inquiry form a key avenue to professional growth. This growth will look different according to the context and the world view of each teacher. Reflection is not always natural; for many it is a learnt skill. It is not always easy. Stepping back from, and questioning, embedded and sometimes routine or expedient behaviours is rarely comfortable. Continual, rigorous reflection is a personal and professional balancing act.

It is also messy. Educators will sometimes ask: 'What does *First Steps* look like in practice?' in the hope that practices might be mimicked. However, *First Steps* is a resource, as opposed to a program, syllabus or curriculum, and as such it is shaped by the nature of the students, the school and community context and by the personal beliefs and understandings that drive teacher practice. What is important is that, in reaching a consensus about direction, teachers in a school engage in vigorous and ongoing debate about their educational beliefs, examining how these beliefs shape learning for students and how they may need to change over time. Teachers, like students, may follow uncommon paths to common outcomes.

Teachers working in different contexts.

First Steps Beliefs

Reflecting on beliefs about teaching, learning and literacy usually has the effect of making these beliefs more tangible. It seems easier to question what certain beliefs look like when they are being enacted in the actual classroom on a daily basis. Reflection of this sort is critical in teaching, given that numerous other factors impact on how things are done. Such factors may include resources, time, expectations and our own personal values about many social and cultural issues. All of these can permeate our teaching and warp intentions. Ongoing reflection on, and owning of established beliefs enable teachers to maintain perspective amid competing priorities.

First Steps beliefs are more a focus for reflection than a set of rules to teach by. They make transparent the theory and ideals that underpin the resource. Teaching, driven by a collection of explicit, positive beliefs, is not necessarily easy but it carries with it intrinsic worth that helps teachers, parents, students and schools understand why something is being done. More importantly it acts as a springboard for action, a cue card for direction and a mirror for reflection. By reflecting on beliefs shared and disputed, teachers can more clearly define why they teach literacy the way they do.

First Steps is based on the belief that effective teaching and learning practice is:

F	Focused on Strategies	**S**	Supportive
I	Investigative	**T**	Tested
R	Reflective	**E**	Embedded
S	Scaffolded	**P**	Purposefully Practised
T	Tailored	**S**	Shared

Figure 3.1

• *Focused on Strategies*

Effective teachers explicitly teach students a range of strategies to create and comprehend texts from a variety of media in a range of contexts. They encourage students to be aware of, apply, monitor and adjust strategies through modelling, guiding and providing practice opportunities across the different curriculum contexts. The ultimate aim is that students will have a bank of known strategies they use independently. They will be able to reflect on the use and effectiveness of strategies as they apply them to different situations.

• *Investigative*

Effective teachers understand that students are active, interactive and hypothesis-driven learners who learn best in investigative or problem-solving situations. They are aware that young children are constantly learning about their environment through interaction, exploration, trial and error, and by 'having a go' at things. As a student's world of experience expands through investigation, deeper understandings are constructed. Effective teachers plan opportunities to engage students in authentic literacy events that require an understanding of purpose, audience and context. Additional learning is always built upon existing foundations, and existing structures are constantly being adapted to accommodate fresh insights.

• *Reflective*

Effective teachers provide time and support for students to reflect, represent and report on their learning in different ways. They show students how to reflect upon their learning to make it more powerful. They understand that students need time to reflect on an experience, on what they have learnt from it and how they learnt it. Often in classrooms busy teachers hustle the students from one learning activity to another, with no time, no space and no structure to help them stand back and think about what they have learnt. Effective teachers realise that if students are encouraged to pause and reflect on the insights they have gained and on things that have started to make sense to them, they will consciously take control of their learning in a new way. Students will develop an awareness of specific understandings and the place of those understandings in the overall scheme of things. They will come to value and respect themselves as learners and will become aware of their own learning processes.

• *Scaffolded*

Effective teachers support students with a range of scaffolds such as modelling, sharing, guiding and conferencing. They use strategic leads and prompts to limit the impact of complex tasks on students' working memory*. Teacher-provided scaffolds are like the trainer wheels on a bike; once the rider has mastered the skill of bike riding the trainer wheels are removed. Scaffolds are seen as interim measures to support student learning in the progress towards independence. Effective teachers provide specific feedback as a key part of this progress.

*Working memory, which is sometimes called M-space, is very different from long- or short-term memory. It is, in effect, a measure of the number of discrete elements which the mind can cope with at any one time.

• Tailored

Effective teachers know that every student progresses along an individual pathway of development. By mapping the milestones of language and literacy development and linking assessment to teaching, effective teachers tailor their teaching to individual, group and class needs. Tailored instruction does not necessarily mean planning and implementing individual learning programs for all students within the classroom. When tailoring instruction, teachers need to look for common needs and develop organisational structures that allow all students to participate at their developmental level. To create a tailored literacy program, effective teachers incorporate a balance of small-group, whole-class and individual instruction.

• Supportive

Effective teachers understand that the learning environment needs to be emotionally safe and receptive to risk-taking. They realise the importance of a constructive, participative and collaborative classroom culture in which students are accepted and supported by their peers, their teacher and the school environment. Effective teachers create an environment in which students feel safe to ask for help when they need it and to express themselves readily without fear of judgement or ridicule.

• Tested

Effective teachers rely heavily on a range of research-based practices that have been thoroughly tested because they know that there is no single method or approach to teach all students successfully. They use their knowledge of current theory, practice and research to guide their selection of appropriate assessment, teaching and learning experiences to help develop the skills and understandings of each individual student in their class. They reflect on the effectiveness of their choices.

• Embedded

Effective teachers embed teaching and learning experiences in the lives of their students, creating contexts across the curriculum that are authentic, socioculturally appropriate and engaging. They plan experiences that build on what they know about their students' development, individual characteristics and cultural background. Effective teachers work to build students' knowledge base both linguistically and conceptually. They help students to make connections between their current understandings and new learning that is being undertaken.

• *Purposefully Practised*

Effective teachers orchestrate purposeful practice over time to help students consolidate and integrate their understandings and skills. They understand that students need to practise and apply a particular aspect of literacy in a number of contexts to develop automaticity. Opportunities to practise in stimulating circumstances constitute an important component of all literacy programs, so that 'mental space' is made available for new learning. The amount of time needed to practise new skills and learning will vary from student to student. Some may need to apply these understandings in only a few situations before they come to terms with them. Others will need to apply the understandings more frequently and in a wider variety of situations before they can begin to generalise and transfer them. In contrast to mindless repetition, purposeful practice is focused, scaffolded and contextualised with an emphasis on process, not product. If the practice is not embedded in, and seen to be arising from, past experience, then only rote learning may occur, while real learning, which is capable of generalisation, will probably not take place. Effective teachers select their practice activities bearing in mind their students' needs and focusing on strategies to be developed.

• *Shared*

Effective teachers understand that real learning occurs when students, teachers, schools and parents share the responsibility of a cohesive learning program and have high expectations. They invite all stakeholders to play pivotal roles in teaching and learning across the curriculum and in everyday life. Effective teachers work collaboratively with support staff to build learning programs that support those students experiencing difficulties within the regular classroom. Whenever a student is withdrawn from the regular classroom to work specifically on a one-on-one basis the program should always be developed in conjunction with the regular classroom literacy program.

CHAPTER 4
First Steps and Diversity

Experience has revealed that *First Steps* can be used successfully with a diverse range of students in many different parts of the world. This success occurs when teachers map the development of their students with factors of diversity such as cultural and linguistic background uppermost in their minds. Similar consideration is given to the selection of Major Teaching Emphases and learning experiences. As a result, teaching is tailored to meet the needs of many different students without marginalising them, or creating an unsustainable teaching load.

Defining Diversity

In an ideal world teachers would respond to the diversity of the students in their care by taking into account every factor that may have an impact on progress at school. These include but are not limited to:
• gender
• age
• cognitive ability
• physical ability
• physical appearance
• learning style
• social background
• economic background
• geographic background
• cultural background
• linguistic background
• religious belief.

All students come to school with diverse literacies and experiences. In any one classroom there may be students who can read and comprehend as competently as students much older than themselves and there may be students who are unable to decode words or comprehend meaningfully. Then there are the others that fall somewhere in between. There are students whose main interest is sport, science, art or a myriad of other subjects. Some students may prefer to work alone while others prefer to work in groups. Some may learn relatively quickly while others may need to have the lesson repeated in different ways many times.

If all students differ in terms of development, interest and learning profiles and if teachers believe their responsibility is to attempt to meet the needs of their students and foster continual growth, then there is no specific teaching methodology that will suit all teachers or all learners. It is necessary, therefore, for teachers to become knowledgeable about their students and find out what students' strengths and competencies are so that appropriate teaching and learning experiences can be chosen.

However, attempts to meet the challenge of diversity by creating individual education plans for each and every student are often impractical and sometimes misguided. A student's learning plan may be developed to respond to the role played by cultural background in learning, but may ignore or minimise consideration of economic circumstances, gender or learning style which influence the individual's learning in equally powerful ways. Similarly, students may be grouped and taught according to a factor of diversity such as English as an Additional Language (EAL), despite the facts that some individuals have quite different experiences with literacy and the group is composed of a range of different language backgrounds. As a result, students may be stereotyped, the teaching focus may be biased and expectations lowered. Assessing, planning and teaching in a way that acknowledges and supports diversity requires ongoing reflection to ensure that students' needs are being met in a practical and effective way.

Catering for Diverse Learners: A Broad Overview

Diverse learners are part of the population of every school. Many of these students are at risk of not achieving their full potential, and the reasons for this are varied.

Teaching for diversity requires that thought be given to what is effective for an individual or group as opposed to isolating certain assessment, teaching and learning practices as 'EAL practices' or 'Gifted and Talented practices'.

For example, research suggests that EAL students generally respond positively to:
- open-ended questions
- opportunities to code-switch
- activities that are highly contextualised
- experiences that value the first language
- tasks that are skilfully scaffolded

- learning experiences that include a reflection component
- visual rather than aural activities.

Gifted and Talented students generally respond positively to:
- open-ended questions and tasks
- negotiated activities
- investigative learning experiences
- opportunities to challenge conventional thinking or approaches
- learning experiences that require the application of multiple abilities and/or cross-curricular subject knowledge.

Although generalised to describe the tendencies of two extremely diverse groups of students, the two lists signal ways of catering for diverse needs in a classroom. By summarising research findings, a generic list of characteristics can be identified. Teachers may create similar lists by summarising research findings on other factors of diversity. Action research in the classroom that focuses on the idiosyncrasies of particular individuals or groups can be used to add to or amend the lists. In this way approaches that may be used for one group of learners may also be useful for others and some practical planning may occur.

The following pages illustrate how approaches, identified through research as most successful with EAL and/or Gifted and Talented students, can also be used with other kinds of learners. It is acknowledged that putting a label on students does not make a homogeneous group. The range of needs and strengths of students within this group will vary significantly. Suggestions on how teachers might use the approaches with different groups are provided.

Catering for Diverse Learners Through Open-ended Questions and Tasks

Catering for Diverse Learners Through Open-ended Questions and Tasks	How Teachers Apply This When Teaching EAL Students	How Teachers Apply This When Teaching Students Experiencing Learning Difficulties in Literacy	How Teachers Apply This When Teaching Gifted and Talented Students
Open-ended questions and tasks require students to think, reflect and communicate effectively. Answering questions gives students an opportunity to demonstrate what they know, whether there are any gaps in their understanding, and their control over language.	Ask questions that allow for discussion and that require more varied and complex sentence structures for the answer.	Encourage students to reflect on their understandings.	Provide opportunities to challenge conventional thinking or approaches; e.g. If you could change this, what would you change it to and why?
Questions such as: What can you tell me about ...? How do you feel about ...? Why do you think ...? are open-ended.	Encourage students to take risks and contribute to discussions.	Use Bloom's *Taxonomy* (or similar) as a guide for developing higher-order thinking skills.	Provide choices in relation to how tasks can be solved and what decisions need to be made.
Open-ended tasks allow students to approach problem-solving in a way they choose as well as demonstrate what they know in their preferred learning style. For example, a student who has investigated weather patterns may demonstrate what they have learnt by using pictures and diagrams if they are a visual learner or by constructing a model if they are a kinaesthetic learner.	Provide opportunities for peer discussion groups; e.g. a reading discussion group will provide students with real opportunities to share stories or books they have read and allow other students to model appropriate language use.	Use a variety of grouping structures so that students have the opportunities to work with other students of varying abilities.	Encourage the use of multiple texts and other supplementary materials.
	Plan activities in which students need to communicate.		Ask questions or set tasks that stimulate inquiry and lead to active exploration and discovery; e.g. What do you think would be the most effective way to ...?

Catering for Diverse Learners Through Activities That Are Heavily Contextualised

Catering for Diverse Learners Through Activities That Are Heavily Contextualised	How Teachers Apply This When Teaching EAL Students	How Teachers Apply This When Teaching Students Experiencing Learning Difficulties in Literacy	How Teachers Apply This When Teaching Gifted and Talented Students
Authentic literacy experiences that have a clear and immediate context enable students to make links with their prior knowledge and expand their knowledge base.	Engage students in activities that enable them to learn both English language and the academic content.	Make all school learning experiences meaningful.	Make use of more complex and abstract materials.
Students need to see the purposes of the tasks in which they are involved and the relevance to their current and future lives. Teachers can assist students to make these connections.	Make the learning context rich, scaffolding the development of English and the concepts being taught.	Use material that is familiar to students; e.g. find music they like and write out song lyrics for a reading task.	Challenge students to develop alternative representations, ideas or applications.
Using language in a meaningful way promotes in students a desire to convey or understand a particular message.	Use real-life scenarios, such as conversations and games when developing talk.	Use material that is capable of attracting and maintaining their attention; e.g. fan magazines, a current news situation of interest and relevance to them.	Encourage students to demonstrate their learning in a wide variety of formats; e.g. instead of preparing a written or oral book report the students could design a game around the themes or characters.
	In order to build a common context, provide a shared experience; e.g. excursion, film, experiment, cooking. Take photos that can be revisited at a later time.	Provide study guides and vocabulary lists before reading.	
	Allow students to read the same book in their home language or watch it on video.	Prepare students for reading and/or writing tasks by activating their prior knowledge; e.g. discuss what they already know about the topic, brainstorm appropriate vocabulary and create graphic organisers.	
	Ensure that students see and hear English being used for specific purposes. This gives them a framework to build on and opportunities to try out and practise new structures.	Use real artefacts (visual, auditory, kinaesthetic) where possible.	

43

Catering for Diverse Learners Through Negotiated Activities

Catering for Diverse Learners Through Negotiated Activities	How Teachers Apply This When Teaching EAL Students	How Teachers Apply This When Teaching Students Experiencing Learning Difficulties in Literacy	How Teachers Apply This When Teaching Gifted and Talented Students
Students are active learners and need the opportunity to take control of their own learning and develop responsibility for their work. This leads to independence. Negotiated learning involves: – shared goal setting between the teacher and student, based on that student's needs and interests – assessment based on student growth and attainment of goals.	Encourage students to choose topics in which they are interested. Give students choices about how to represent their learning; e.g. write a report, build a model, draw pictures or do an oral presentation. Assist students to make choices that will develop their skills and understandings. Encourage collaboration with students of similar interests.	Encourage self-motivation by allowing students some choice about the learning experiences they undertake. Provide support by creating a negotiated curriculum based on individual or small-group needs. Support learners in reaching the goals they have set for themselves. Allow for a variety of grouping arrangements where the students can choose whom to work with and for how long. Provide a variety of games that allow purposeful practice of skills and understandings.	Provide a challenging and enriched curriculum. Encourage cooperation and collaboration on tasks. Provide opportunities for inquiry-based studies; e.g. allow students to examine an area of interest and decide on a problem or topic to study in depth. Encourage students to undertake experiences that develop their strengths and interests. Allow students to take control of their learning and set realistic goals to develop independence as learners.

Catering for Diverse Learners Through Visual and Aural Activities

Catering for Diverse Learners Through Visual and Aural Activities	How Teachers Apply This When Teaching EAL Students	How Teachers Apply This When Teaching Students Experiencing Learning Difficulties in Literacy	How Teachers Apply This When Teaching Gifted and Talented Students
Using visual and/or concrete artefacts enables students to build up their background knowledge and make connections between spoken, visual and written language. Learning may proceed more smoothly when a student can integrate the senses rather than just relying on the aural.	Provide pictures, photos, drawings, charts and diagrams to support talk. Encourage the use of gestures and body language. Create opportunities for students to use multimedia. Record oral discussions; e.g. brainstorming to reinforce learning. Use demonstrations and activities where students have the opportunity for 'hands-on' learning. Combine visual with aural activities; e.g. highlight the visual pattern as well as identifying the appropriate sound when teaching spelling patterns.	Students have preferred ways of learning. Providing opportunities for students to demonstrate what they know in a form they choose can be empowering.	

Catering for Diverse Learners Through Experiences That Value the First Language

Catering for Diverse Learners Through Experiences That Value the First Language	How Teachers Apply This When Teaching EAL Students	How Teachers Apply This When Teaching Students Experiencing Learning Difficulties in Literacy	How Teachers Apply This When Teaching Gifted and Talented Students
The home language of students must be valued within the school context. Allowing students to see their language and culture honoured can empower them, help boost their self-esteem and confidence, encourage them to be risk-takers and provide positive school experiences.	Provide opportunities for students to read, write or speak with others in their first language.	Unless these students also have English as an additional language this section is not applicable.	
	Encourage the development of books and tapes for students to read or listen to in their home language.		
	Include in the school newsletter stories students have written in their home language.		
	Study the different cultures of students and celebrate or acknowledge cultural events.		
	Use literature, music and art from students cultures.		
	Encourage parent/community involvement and assistance.		
	Create environmental print that incorporates students languages as well as English.		

Using *First Steps* with Diverse Learners

Teachers can use *First Steps* resources to support diverse learners. The *First Steps* materials have a variety of features that assist teachers to support these learners successfully. The materials:

• allow for the identification of varied patterns of development
• provide scope to annotate Maps of Development
• provide support for teachers to differentiate instruction
• assist teachers to select from a wide range of effective teaching and learning practices
• include activities and learning experiences that are adaptable.

Identification of Varied Patterns of Development

The *First Steps* Maps of Development collectively provide a framework for recording students' literacy development. Although the Maps of Development are based on research and theory generated in English-speaking contexts, many of these contexts include student populations that are culturally, linguistically and cognitively diverse. In using the Maps of Development to ascertain a student's progress, teachers need to be aware that such diversity means that there is no such thing as a 'normal' profile. Each student will display an individual pathway that may include quiet or slow periods of development and periods of rapid growth. Regardless of the pattern of development that emerges, it is vital that teachers continue to reflect on why particular indicators have been displayed and what role has been played by one or more factors of diversity.

There is no requirement that a student begin at the first phase on a Map of Development and show progress to the final phase. For example, students who bring to school literacy experiences in a language other than English will be unlikely to engage in 'pretend reading' behaviours because they are aware of many concepts of print. Instead they may draw on those understandings to display indicators further along the Map of Development. In this situation it may be helpful to record the literacy behaviours they display in their other language as well as in English. In contrast, a student with a disability or learning difficulty may display indicators in quite advanced phases in one substrand, but not in another, due to the nature of the disability or difficulty. The purpose of the Map of Development is to reveal these patterns so teachers can tailor their instruction rather than label students with a phase name for reporting purposes.

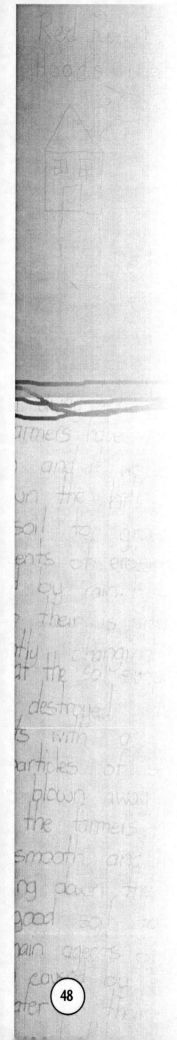

Scope to Annotate Maps of Development

Teachers can annotate individual students' Maps of Development, noting such elements of diversity as:
- the nature of the student; e.g. 'used a communication aid'
- the instructional setting; e.g. 'worked in a group to complete task'
- the sociocultural setting; e.g. directionality of how print is written and read in first language differs from English.

By undertaking action research, liaising with peers, discussing with parents and reflecting on research findings, teachers may also be able to note additional behaviours that are consistently displayed by particular students but not included in the indicators of the *First Steps* Map of Development.

Consider the case of a teacher working with a student who has English as an additional language or dialect. The student may have difficulty representing all vowel and consonant sounds due to the effect of a first language or dialect, e.g. omitting inflectional endings when spelling certain words. By identifying the prevalence and consistency of the behaviour, discussing it with the student's previous teacher, reflecting on the appropriateness of the teaching the student has encountered, and examining the research available on the topic, the teacher may choose to add the behaviour on the individual's Map of Development. Generalising this behaviour to other students who have English as an additional language or dialect would be risky. Especially when the nature of the first language or dialect of some students may not have the same effect on that particular literacy behaviour.

Support for Teachers to Differentiate Instruction

The *First Steps* materials have been designed to help teachers link assessment to teaching for a range of students. The Major Teaching Emphases help teachers to tailor instruction for individual, small-group and whole-class teaching. Guidelines for decision-making are also provided in areas such as assessment procedures, grouping of students and the selection of texts. There are no foolproof ways of catering for diverse needs, but research and experience provide a basis for the consideration of many factors. Similarly there is no replacement for the professional judgement that is used to apply these understandings to each educational context encountered.

Selection from a Wide Range of Effective Teaching and Learning Practices

The *Linking Assessment, Teaching and Learning* Book identifies Effective Teaching and Learning Practices that have been made explicit to assist teachers in expanding and refining their teaching repertoire. These practices are elaborated in each Resource Book as teaching procedures specific to that strand. The selection and use of these practices and procedures allows teachers to cater for diverse learners. While the list of practices and procedures is not exhaustive, the overt discussion and application of each is designed to help teachers reflect on which teaching and learning approaches work best for which students, and for what reason.

Activities and Learning Experiences That Are Adaptable

Suggested teaching and learning experiences are included at each phase of the Map of Development Books and as generic experiences in the Resource Books. The learning experiences have been written in such a way that they are not content- or text-specific. This allows for adaptation to meet the needs of diverse student groups. Research has indicated high levels of effectiveness where an educational program is culturally inclusive and responsive*. For example, students from cultures with prominent oral storytelling traditions often perform better when asked to demonstrate their comprehension through retelling, rather than answering a series of disconnected questions. Opportunities for the use of a first language or dialect, such as using technology to make the experience accessible to those with disabilities, or ways of extending the task to make it more challenging for the talented and gifted can be considered. The suggested learning experiences are not an exhaustive list, but a springboard for the generation of further activities that would be appropriate to meet student needs.

Using *First Steps* with Diverse Learners: Case Stories

The *First Steps* resource has been used successfully, for over a decade, with diverse students in many different parts of the world. While the beliefs underpinning *First Steps* stay the same, the implementation and use of the resource has been adapted to suit the needs of individual students and the school environment. This section provides a snapshot of how five teachers, from different contexts, have successfully used *First Steps* with their students.

• Case Story 1: Using *First Steps* with Students for Whom English
            Is an Additional Language (EAL)

---

*Vogt, L., Jordan, C. and Tharp, R. (1987), Explaining school failure, producing school success: Two cases, *Anthropology and Education Quarterly*, 18, pp. 276–86.

- Case Story 2: Using *First Steps* with Students Experiencing Learning Difficulties

- Case Story 3: Using *First Steps* with Geographically Isolated Students

- Case Story 4: Using *First Steps* with Deaf Students

- Case Story 5: Using *First Steps* with Adult Learners

Note: The photos in this section are generic in nature and not specific to the Case Stories recorded here.

Case Story 1: Using First Steps with Students for Whom English Is an Additional Language (EAL)

Teacher: Margaret
Context: International School, Germany

My group of Grade 2 EAL learners consists of seven Korean children aged from seven to nine years. All of them are literate in Korean and demonstrate their knowledge by, for example, reading the Korean version of 'Cinderella'. The students all know and use the Roman alphabet.

The language of instruction for these students is now English. After assessing the daily journal writing they had been doing in their home-rooms as well as their writing in my EAL class, I determined that all students were in the Early Writing Phase on the *First Steps* Developmental Continuum (now known as Maps of Development). The Major Teaching Emphases from this phase pointed me in the direction of focusing on the structure and organisation of a range of text forms. I embarked on a series of lessons using fairytales to help improve their narrative writing. Since they already knew the stories, the fairytales provided learning contexts that did not burden the students' working memory. These texts also provided authentic situations in which to practise the past-tense form of verbs and the language of time. These students needed this for sequencing and expanding their simple sentence structures. I selected procedures and activities from the *First Steps* resources that I knew would support the Major Teaching Emphases as well as the school's curriculum objectives.

In a shared reading session we explored the text 'Cinderleela', an adaptation of the Cinderella story. In a whole-class activity we located the expressions of time in the text and recorded these for ongoing reference. We practised using these orally, trying to remember where they came in the text and using the relevant tense. We expanded some of these time phrases into our own personal contexts. At a later date we used the time phrases in some sentence manipulation activities based on the 'Cinderleela' story. We looked at sequencing, interchangeability and the degree of precision of these time words and phrases. The Principal sat in on that particular lesson and was extremely impressed by the amount and quality of the language being generated by these EAL beginners now in their fourth month of learning English.

The *First Steps* resources provided me with guiding principles to support language and literacy development of my EAL students. I am grateful that EAL teachers and home-room teachers are now, with the help of *First Steps*, speaking the same language in describing the progress of our shared students.

Case Story 2: Using First Steps *with Students Experiencing Learning Difficulties*

Teacher: Jacqui
Context: Primary School, Australia

My school is located in a low to middle socio–economic area in Perth and currently has over 800 students. In my present class I have twenty-eight students, two-thirds of whom are boys. They are a diverse group of students representing a wide range of ability, where one-third would be considered 'at risk'.

This year I have one student who was diagnosed eighteen months ago with dyslexia. This student has difficulties with visual and auditory memory, and subsequently has reading, writing and spelling problems. Little progress has been made in literacy over the past three years. I use *First Steps* in conjunction with specific strategies aimed at addressing the needs of students with dyslexia to construct appropriate learning programs. At the beginning of the year, I conducted several assessment tasks to determine development in Reading, Writing and Spelling. This information was recorded on the *First Steps* Developmental Continua (now known as Maps of Development). From this information I developed an 'Individual Education Plan' that focused on helping the student to achieve particular goals (see Figure 4.1 on page 54). I located appropriate teaching and learning experiences in the *First Steps* resources, making modifications where necessary.

I adapted the Spelling Journal approach from *First Steps* to ensure two words of personal choice as well as three words from the 'Bedrock Sight Vocabulary' list were learnt. It is important for dyslexic students to continually revise previously learnt words so I ensured that the words were put on a two-weekly rotation so they could be revisited regularly. A multi-sensory approach to learning to spell is particularly successful for students with dyslexia. I therefore used the 'Eight-Step Spelling Strategy' in which the student gained practice in seeing, hearing, writing, and saying aloud the spelling words. Using a 'Have-a-Go' pad has been beneficial in helping to develop visual memory and for trying out different ways of spelling unknown words.

A successful *First Steps* approach for supporting writing has been the use of writing frameworks. To begin, the student was supported with sequencing paragraphs in a logical order, and then to elicit the structure of the particular text type to construct a writing framework. The frameworks provide a vital scaffold for early attempts at creating written texts and have made a significant difference to this student's writing development. Charts of the various writing frameworks displayed in the classroom to refer to when needed are also extremely useful.

It was important that any writing activities were manageable so that the student could experience success. Dictating texts onto an audiotape, and then having another student or parent volunteer scribe it onto the computer was valuable. Other activities that proved successful included:
• teaching the appropriate use of the spell-check facility on the computer
• using negotiated editing; e.g. indicating the number of errors in particular lines of text for the student to locate.

Being dyslexic the student had become overly concerned with 'sounding out' as a major word-attack strategy. Shared reading was an effective procedure for developing other word-identification strategies through teacher modelling. Using cloze activities with a variety of texts also supported the development of other efficient strategies to work out unknown words.

Encouraging the use of the 'Five Finger Strategy' when choosing texts to read for pleasure has enabled the student to become more independent.

I have found using the *First Steps* Developmental Continua (Maps of Development) to record progress and determine appropriate strategies, in conjunction with specific dyslexia strategies, to be invaluable. It can appear to dyslexic students that they are showing little improvement. The *First Steps* indicators have enabled me to demonstrate to this student that progress is being made. The indicators also provided a guide for developing small achievable goals that were discussed in regular student–teacher conferences. By reviewing these goals the student could see what progress had been made and what to focus on next. The *First Steps* Developmental Continua (Maps of Development) were also helpful when discussing development with the student's parents. These, together with explicit teaching strategies and supportive frameworks within *First Steps* make it an effective resource to use with dyslexic students.

INDIVIDUAL EDUCATION PLAN: LITERACY

Student: Year

At/Below Benchmark: Writing *No*   Reading *No*   Spelling *Yes*   First Steps Phases: *Reading* - Early   *Writing* - Early   *Spelling* - Phonetic

Relevant Learning Needs: dyslexia; wears glasses and needs to sit facing the blackboard, and close to the front of the class

Focus First Steps Indicators:

Reading:
- Is becoming efficient in the use of the following word identification strategies for constructing meaning: sounds out to decode words; uses initial letters; uses knowledge of common letter patterns; uses known parts of words to make sense of whole word; uses blending and word segmentation; uses syllabification

Writing:
- Writes a range of text forms including stories, reports, procedures and expositions
- Uses a variety of simple and compound sentences

Spelling:
- Is beginning to use visual strategies, such as knowledge of common letter patterns and critical features of words

Major Teaching Emphases:

Reading:
- Model strategies for attacking unknown words eg. Identifying similar word beginnings, common word patterns, chunking parts of a word

Writing:
- Read, write and discuss a range of different forms of writing for different purposes and audiences

Spelling:
- Model the use of appropriate linking words
- Teach writers to look for visual patterns and common letter sequences in words; and to identify critical features of words

Teaching and Learning Strategies:

Spelling	Writing	Reading
• Use 8 Step Spelling multisensory strategy to learn new focus words	• Sequence sentences to reconstruct various text types and elicit genre frameworks	• Daily Flash cards of Bedrock sight words
• Introduce 'Walton' chart to structure learning of graphophonic relationships. Focus on Unexpected sounds – ch, sh, th, wh, qu, -ng, -nk and blends – beginning and end of words	• Model writing of narrative, recount and exposition.	• Listening Post – 'Too Cool' books with text to follow
	• Provide genre frameworks as scaffolds for writing. Display on class charts	• Teach 'Five Finger' strategy for choosing reading texts
• Play 'sound clues' – say sound of blend and a clue eg. say bl and 'a colour' = blue	• Build sentences using adjectives, adverbs. Use sentence maker incorporating focus sight words	• Predict content before reading, activate prior knowledge of topic
• Rainbow colour – give each phoneme a different colour and practise the colour letters, then join together	• Write two sentences based on class text, and use computer to draft sentences	• Prompt with word identification strategies during reading – read on, reread, substitute, initial letter, sound out
• Say the blends – write word on board, underline the blends, read aloud and fill in the blend	• Use picture maps and construct a sentence to describe each main event	• Model reading of multisyllabic words using steps outlined in Walton text
• Sound blocks – one block for each sound, match letter(s) to sounds heard	• Finish the sentence – use examples from reader	• Picture map of story and use for oral retell
• Make words with play dough	• Develop fluent, linked handwriting style	• Cloze activities on own text
• Build 'word family' lists – common visual patterns	• Dictate text onto audio tape for transcribing by parent volunteer	• Scribe own language in stories and focus on basic sight words
• Play 'What comes next?' using focus letter pattern words		• Find words in a text with particular letter patterns
• Play 'Snap' matching words with same visual patterns		• List words that rhyme with chosen focus word
• Use 'Error cues' when proofreading own writing		• Model self-questioning when reading

Figure 4.1: Sample Individual Education Plan: Literacy

Case Story 3: Using First Steps with Geographically Isolated Students

Teacher: Bette
Context: Distance Learning, Australia

For the last six years I have worked in a team-teaching situation at the Schools of Isolated and Distance Education (SIDE). This centre services students who, for a variety of reasons, are unable to attend a 'regular' school. My teaching partner and I have up to forty-three students in all grades from Kindergarten to Year 7, a number of them being family groups. These students are situated all over the world. A small group are in isolated situations in the southern sector of Western Australia, some are on yachts, a number are travelling around Australia and another group is in various overseas locations due to parental work commitments.

In the majority of cases the parents, using lesson plans developed by the SIDE writing team, tutor these students. These lessons form the basis of the curriculum. Many of the *First Steps* strategies have been incorporated in the writing of the curriculum materials, e.g. use of the *First Steps* writing frameworks. The parents, very few of whom have a formal teaching background, supervise the completion of the lessons and ensure they are returned to us on a regular basis. Many of our students return their work via computer with accompanying digital photos, video clips and sound files. We communicate with the students via computer, phone or post at frequent intervals.

I have used the *First Steps* Developmental Continua (now known as Maps of Development) to determine each student's level of development. This has allowed me to adjust our lesson plans/curriculum to suit their particular developmental level. *First Steps* has also been an invaluable tool in assisting parents to understand where their children are in their literacy development and what to do to move them along. I have used the Indicators, Teaching Strategies, Behaviours To Be Encouraged and the 'For Parents' pages from the relevant phases to create a parent guide. I also regularly share materials from the 'Parents as Partners' book as support material. The *First Steps* materials give both parents and students assurance and practical strategies which they can implement no matter what their particular situation.

Case Story 4: Using First Steps *with Deaf Students*

Teacher: Heather
Context: School for the Deaf, United States of America

Education is a challenging profession. Teachers must constantly adapt to the populations in their classrooms. Deaf Education brings an added set of challenges. Educators of deaf and hard-of-hearing students must bring rich learning opportunities while balancing a range of communication styles.

Our school serves a broad range of deaf and hard-of-hearing students with diverse learning styles. In order to meet the variety of needs within this English-language-challenged population, teachers did a self-study of methods, practices and materials used in classrooms. After this, a committee of teachers researched several resources for reading instruction. The decision was then made to implement *First Steps*, as it met the needs identified by our teachers. These included:
- guidelines
- support to focus on student needs rather than 'age/year level' teaching
- structure with flexibility to use a variety of materials
- a teacher-friendly resource
- a variety of activities and strategies
- a resource that promoted consistency among the wide variety of student needs and instructional styles within the school.

The concept of Developmental Learning has mirrored the developmental needs of this particular population of students. Placing the focus on phases of learning rather than grade levels has given the students opportunities to reach levels of success at their own pace. Because teachers created the *First Steps* resource, the appeal is evident. Teachers understand what other teachers need. The wide variety of friendly, fun activities and support has given our educators a wealth of instructional methods to choose from.

The elementary teachers in our school have completed both the Reading and Writing components of the *First Steps* professional development. The upper-level instructors started with the *First Steps* Reading professional development. This has formed a transitional bridge for students as they graduate from the Lower School to the Upper School. It has also provided opportunities for interaction between teachers from Pre-K through to twelfth grade. Future plans include continued professional development and ongoing support so the school, as a whole, speaks the same '*First Steps* language'.

Case Story 5: Using First Steps with Adult Learners

Teacher: Nigel
Context: Basic Skills Adult Education, United Kingdom

Much of the work I do in Basic Skills Adult Education (Family Learning) is delivering short courses in Literacy (or Numeracy). Hence, the learners tend to be parents whose own experience of school was not good and who now want to improve their own basic skills and support their children's learning. I also work with asylum seeker families with limited English. Some of these adults have excellent literacy skills in their first languages; others do not.

I know that *First Steps* is a literacy resource that was developed primarily for school-aged learners, but I have found it invaluable in working with all the adult groups. My teaching has been very much influenced by what I learnt during the *First Steps* professional development. For example, I use modelling, letting students discover 'rules' for themselves and am always aware of PEWIT (Problem Solving, Embeddedness, Working Memory, Interaction, Time)!

I adapt *First Steps* activities as necessary for adult learners, but many activities can be used just as they are. 'Word Back Spied Her', for example, always goes down well and is a great way of highlighting subject-specific or key words. Adapted versions of 'Crazy Cloze' have had some groups giggling for hours. Yes, some activities are even better played with adults!

I have found that spelling is the thing that many of the parent learners are anxious about. I draw heavily on the materials and suggestions from the *First Steps* Spelling resources. It is amazing how quickly these learners gain confidence when they realise, for example, that they can spell most of a word.

I use the *First Steps* Developmental Continua (now Maps of Development) as a guide for my own teaching. I also draw on the Continua when talking to parents about their children's literacy development and things they can do to support their child at home. I share this information with them through discussion and sometimes provide a brief handout.

I can honestly say that *First Steps* has made an enormous difference to the way that I approach teaching literacy. It continues to be a real support for me, no matter who the learners are. My own son has a severe learning difficulty and I know that *First Steps* has given me both insights and tools to help his development, too. *First Steps* even impacts on teaching numeracy—the principles of PEWIT are just as valid there.

CHAPTER 5
Establishing a Positive Teaching and Learning Environment

The Importance of a Positive Teaching and Learning Environment

A visitor to a stranger's home gets a sense of what is important to the inhabitants, and how things are done in that household. The introduction of fellow members of the household implies respect; the display of homemade artwork conveys a sense of pride and accomplishment; and the nature of the activity in the house suggests the interests of individuals. A classroom community is no different. Students, teachers, parents and community visitors enter, thinking:

• What is important here?

• How are things done?

• Who constructed this environment?

• Why are things the way they are?

Teacher beliefs about how students learn provide the basis for the kinds of learning environment established in classrooms. Although many teachers share common beliefs and philosophies about learning, classrooms rarely look or sound the same. Individual teachers and students shape the environment to support their own particular needs. Translating beliefs into practice involves teachers in making decisions about their own teaching and the social and physical environment of the classroom.

Reflecting *First Steps* Beliefs in Creating a Positive Teaching and Learning Environment

Creating a positive environment that promotes social, emotional and academic excellence is vitally important if students are to succeed. The beliefs underpinning *First Steps* provide a sound basis for making decisions about the physical setting and the culture of the classroom.

As emphasised in Chapter 3, *First Steps* is based on the beliefs that the practice of effective teaching and learning is:

F	Focused on Strategies	**S**	Supportive
I	Investigative	**T**	Tested
R	Reflective	**E**	Embedded
S	Scaffolded	**P**	Purposefully Practised
T	Tailored	**S**	Shared

The following pages illustrate how the creation of a positive teaching and learning environment is influenced by these beliefs.

Focused on Strategies

Effective teachers explicitly teach students a range of strategies to create and comprehend texts from a variety of media in a range of contexts. They encourage students to be aware of, apply, monitor and adjust strategies through modelling, guiding, and providing practice opportunities and application across the different curriculum contexts.

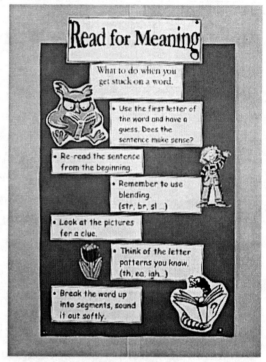

Sample of collaboratively generated classroom strategy chart

A teaching and learning environment focused on strategies may include:

- students referring to collaboratively generated (teacher and students) charts that provide guidelines about use of strategies; e.g. 'How to spell a difficult word', 'Ways to check that I'm making sense when reading' or 'Being an effective listener'
- the teacher recapping a strategy by writing the lesson objective
- pieces of student work on display, annotated with teacher feedback about the effective use of strategies as opposed to a generic comment such as 'Nice work, Lina'
- opportunities for students to reflect on and discuss their use of strategies with others
- opportunities to discuss how strategies have been applied across the learning areas.

Investigative

Effective teachers understand that students are active, interactive and hypothesis-driven learners who learn best in investigative or problem-solving situations. They are aware that young children are constantly learning about their environment through interaction, exploration, trial and error, and through 'having a go' at things.

> **An investigative teaching and learning environment may include:**
> - places and items that provoke cross-curriculum inquiry and use of language; e.g. an aquarium, a miniature greenhouse or a set of balance scales
> - places and items that provoke literacy-focused inquiry linked to other learning areas; e.g. a computer connected to the Internet, an audio-taped reading of an excerpt from a novel or a daily newspaper article located on a world map
> - open-ended tasks as part of daily activities
> - time to discuss and record probing, higher-order questions and reflections about places and items of investigation
> - opportunities to work collaboratively with peers; e.g. working in small groups to produce a Readers' Theatre, working in pairs to research a topic on the Internet
> - learning charts that demonstrate ongoing inquiry and capture the developing understandings and thoughts of students
> - learning opportunities that promote risk-taking and acceptance of multiple possibilities in responses.

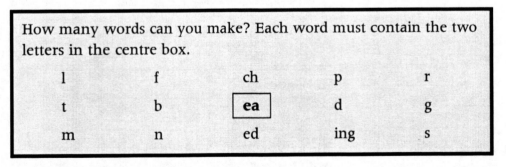

How many words can you make? Each word must contain the two letters in the centre box.

l	f	ch	p	r
t	b	**ea**	d	g
m	n	ed	ing	s

Figure 5.1: Example of open-ended task

Reflective

Effective teachers provide time and support for students to reflect, represent and report on their learning in different ways. They show students how to reflect upon their learning to make it more powerful. They understand that students need time to reflect on an experience, on what they have learnt from it and how they learnt this.

A reflective teaching and learning environment may include:

- a quiet area for small-group conferences where students can share their work and respond to suggestions
- 'Have-a-Go' pads on desks so that students can rehearse their spelling and reflect on their attempts
- cumulative charts that represent ongoing learning
- open-ended questions posed freely by students in response to a focus
- self-talk or 'thinking aloud' as a means of clarifying and consolidating new understandings and skills
- a time to share new discoveries and look back at what worked and what didn't, with a particular focus on strategies
- the use of reflection processes and the products of reflection such as learning logs or journals.

I Pat the soil into the
Pot. the soil is black the soil.
to get all the roots away.
I watered the Pot.

Figure 5.2a: Independent writing sample from Year 1 student

Thinking About Your Writing

Name: _Nick_   Date: _18.9.07_

1. I found this piece of writing *Easy* *(Difficult)* (circle one)

2. The best part of this piece of writing is _that I put in lots of the right words and letters._

I did this by _sounding out and remembering how to spell the "buzz" words (sight words)._

3. Something I want to work on for the future is _putting finger spacing in my writing_

I plan to do this by _putting my finger next to one word and then doing the next word after that._

Figure 5.2b: Writer's reflection sheet completed with teacher

Scaffolded

Effective teachers support students with a range of scaffolds such as modelling, sharing, guiding and conferencing. They use strategic leads and prompts to limit the impact of complex tasks on students' working memory.

A scaffolded teaching and learning environment may include:

- an area for whole-class and small-group modelled, shared and guided lessons
- collaboratively-generated (teacher and students) charts that provide working guidelines for the completion of tasks; e.g. **writing of specific text types**
- differentiated tasks being assigned as part of daily activities
- spaces and procedures for conducting conferences
- student-generated word banks
- appropriate technology to support all students; e.g. **voice-activated computer**
- time for peer tutoring and collaboration
- time for all students to work with the teacher
- opportunities for students to work in a variety of groupings.

Teacher scaffolding for students by recording a whole-class brainstorm

Tailored

Effective teachers know that every student progresses along an individual pathway of development. By mapping the milestones of language and literacy development and linking assessment to teaching, effective teachers tailor their teaching to individual, group and class needs.

A tailored teaching and learning environment may include:
- a seating arrangement that enables students to move easily to individual, paired, small-group or whole-class settings
- materials for a wide range of ability levels
- learning centres or sites containing activities that challenge a range of senses and learning styles; e.g. **moveable letters, audio-taped poems, language games, computers**
- an area to display self-generated or negotiated literacy goals
- learning experiences that cater for a range of learning styles and developmental levels.

A display of self-generated literacy goals tailored for each student

Supportive

Effective teachers understand that the learning environment needs to be emotionally safe and receptive to risk-taking. They realise the importance of a constructive, participative and collaborative classroom culture in which students are accepted and supported by their peers, their teacher and the school environment.

A supportive teaching and learning environment may include:

- collaboratively generated (teacher and students) charts at eye level that list an agreed code of behaviour, roles or students' rights and responsibilities
- Y- or T- charts that describe what positive social behaviours look, feel and sound like
- a safe place for storing students' belongings
- prominent and frequently changing displays of students' work
- students asking more questions than the teacher
- students contributing freely and comfortably to discussions, including constructive criticism
- processes and products such as codes of behaviour and favourite-topic surveys that have been generated at class meetings
- students being encouraged to take, and rewarded for taking, risks.

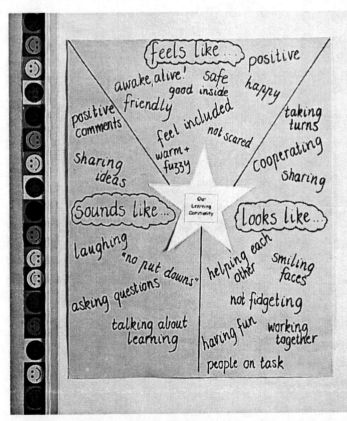

A class-generated Y-chart describing positive social behaviours

Tested

Effective teachers rely heavily on a range of research-based practices that have been thoroughly tested because they know that there is no single method or approach to successfully teach all students. They use their knowledge of current theory, practice and research to guide their selection of appropriate assessment, as well as teaching and learning experiences to help develop the skills and understandings of each individual student in their class.

A teaching and learning environment designed around approaches that have been tested may include:

- teaching practices that are underpinned by research and reflective of teachers' beliefs
- teachers willing to try new strategies, reflect on their success and reconcile this thinking with what reliable research says
- a variety of instructional practices and procedures
- a shared reason for doing things; e.g. 'The 200 words in our common word bank make up 68 per cent of the words most people write. We need to be able to spell these easily.'

A teacher scans current literacy publications.

A teacher searches the Web for information about current literacy practices.

Embedded

Effective teachers embed teaching and learning experiences in the lives of their students, creating contexts across the curriculum that are authentic, socioculturally appropriate and engaging. They plan experiences that build on what they know about their students' development, individual characteristics and cultural background.

A teaching and learning environment with embedded learning experiences may include:

- work displays that include the first language or dialect, or cultural displays
- charts that are covered in examples of text forms collected by students as they have become familiar with the form
- texts that reflect students' interests, cross-curricular topics and diverse cultures
- a calendar that includes festivals and celebrations of a wide range of religions and cultures
- adaptations to work and traffic areas to assist students with disabilities or special needs
- displays that include student names alongside home and community achievements
- a range of visitors from the local community.

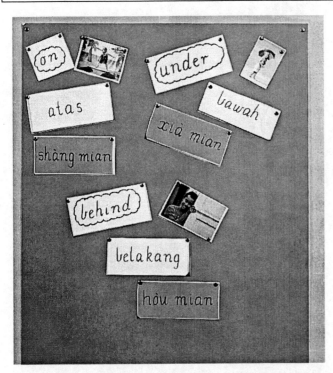

A classroom display incorporating students' first languages

Purposefully Practised

Effective teachers orchestrate purposeful practice over time to help students consolidate and integrate their understandings and skills. They understand that students need to practise and apply a particular aspect of literacy in a number of contexts to develop proficiency.

A teaching and learning environment that encourages purposeful practice may include:

- a selection of games and activities that promote the consolidation of skills and understandings
- small learning centres equipped with tools to encourage practice
- small copies of known big books made available for individual student use
- time allocated to practise new skills and strategies across learning areas.

A student uses the writing centre to practise new skills.

Shared

Effective teachers understand that learning occurs when students, teachers, schools and parents share the responsibility of a cohesive learning program and have high expectations. They invite all stakeholders to play pivotal roles in teaching and learning across the curriculum and in everyday life.

A teaching and learning environment that promotes shared responsibility may include:

- a space for parent helpers to sit and discuss work with students
- a display of school initiatives, such as fund-raising or community events
- home–school communication books
- a shared letter to or from a community member on a whiteboard or flip-chart
- 'parent nights' where students take their parents and/or carers on learning journeys
- a roster of responsibilities (may include teachers, students, helpers, principal)
- a two-way message board or mailbox that holds brief positive messages
- provision of time for student self-assessment and goal-setting
- opportunities to work collaboratively with others; e.g. **peer tutoring, buddy classes**
- teachers working as teams
- students conducting class meetings.

An opportunity to work collaboratively with a partner

The Physical Environment

This section of the chapter looks at ways teachers can create and enhance the teaching and learning environment for their students with a focus on the physical environment.

Factors to Consider

As each new school year starts, teachers around the world spend hours thinking about how to set up their classrooms effectively. What and how the teacher is expecting students to learn will affect the physical layout of the room. It makes sense to have an environment that is comfortable, stimulating and attractive as these factors are conducive to learning. Walking into a classroom that is visually rich can be appealing to students. However, if teachers want their students to use this resource on a daily basis, the students need to have some ownership of what is displayed. Collaboratively generating and building the print-rich classroom environment over time is a powerful approach to understanding how literacy works.

When deciding on the layout of the classroom, effective teachers take into account the classroom culture they wish to promote and the needs of their students. Considering the physical arrangement of the classroom—where to have a meeting area; how chairs and tables are arranged; where the equipment and materials are kept— will all facilitate implementation of different activities and the accommodation of different working groups. For example, while desks in rows facing the front might imply that the teacher dominates the instructional process, the arrangement also reflects an understanding of the importance of attending behaviours and active listening. Students can easily form groups of four by turning their desks around and joining the pair behind them. Teachers should consider changing the physical layout of the room throughout the year according to the social dynamics of the class, the nature of the teaching and learning, and their own professional reflection.

When planning the physical layout of a classroom consider the following factors.

- **Fixed Features**

  What in the way of doors, windows, permanent cupboards and display boards cannot be moved?

- **Climate**

  What areas will be affected by heating, cooling, or wind?

- **Traffic**

  Is there adequate access to exits, storage and meeting areas?

- **Noise**

  Is there sufficient space between quiet areas and noisy areas?

- **Student Numbers**

  Which areas are designed for working alone, in pairs, as a group, as a whole class?

- **Supervision**

  Can the teacher easily see the students?

- **Furniture**

  Is the available furniture appropriate for the activity?

- **Safety**

  Does the classroom have any features or furniture that pose a health or safety risk?

- **Student Attention**

  Do the arrangements encourage on-task behaviour?

- **Proximity**

  Are adjoining areas compatible? That is, should a hands-on art area be next to a computer area?

Organising Floor Areas

There are many ways to go about organising the physical setting of the classroom. One way is to consider the room from a bird's-eye view, allocating areas according to needs. An approximate bird's-eye view of the classroom should begin with a draft plan that shows fixed features. (If this is done during the school year, students might be able to help construct the diagram and assist with the decision-making.) Small squares or adhesive notes can then be used to represent the main areas required in the room. Areas need not be substantial. An area could simply be a learning centre housed on a small table in a corner.

Consider the following areas and their purposes.

Area	Purpose: To Accommodate...
Teacher's area	Desk, display board and storage
Students' desk area	Chairs and desks for conventional seatwork
Instruction area	Whole-class and small-group gatherings; e.g. modelled and shared lessons, class meetings
Quiet area	Recreational reading
Computer area	Computer-based tasks—using software, CD-ROMs, Internet
Activity area	Interactive materials for investigation
Wet area	Art and science work where a tap and sink are required
Learning Centre area	A focus on a strand, a theme or a skill
Personal storage area	Bags, lunches and other personal items
Listening Post area	Headsets for listening to taped books and spoken texts
Calm-down or time-out area	Students who have become distressed or frustrated, and require time and space to regain their composure

Inevitably, areas will be shaped according to the space and furniture available, and the teaching and learning preferences of the teacher and students. One way is to move the areas around the room and consider each arrangement in the light of the ten factors influencing the layout of the classroom (see previous page). Some areas may be adapted or merged and new areas created. Although many permutations may be tried it is unlikely a plan will result that doesn't include some potential for friction. If teachers are aware of this potential, however, it can be managed. Some areas may require boundaries to maximise their effectiveness; e.g. **a mat to mark an instruction area**. Areas will often serve multiple purposes. The instruction area, as the largest open space in the room, may be appropriate for small group meetings and limited physical activities such as stretching.

Ms Bellatoni: Year 4 Class Plan

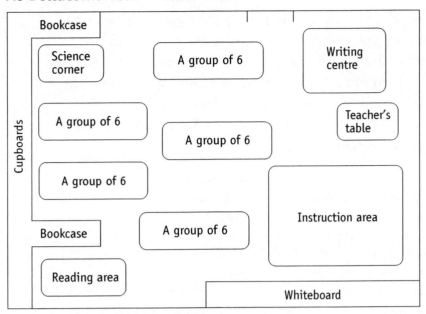

Figure 5.2: Draft plan for classroom arrangement

Furniture and features can often be adapted to meet the needs of students. For example, most young students don't appear to mind sitting on the floor, whereas some older students find it a little demeaning. Some teachers will simply pull their chairs across to instruct or read to their students, yet others have rejuvenated a large old armchair and endowed it with all sorts of powers to motivate their students. Visiting other classrooms, viewing teacher resource books and watching home improvement shows will provide inspiration for areas with theme and character, making them attractive and multi-dimensional yet functional. For example, an early-childhood Listening Post becomes an octopus or a spider studio, or an old sofa is signposted, 'For Literature Lizards Only' and accompanied by a cartoon of a reptile reading. The idea is to give areas prominence and atmosphere by decorating according to a theme, designating boundaries with furniture and creating a sense of privilege in the use of that area.

'Anything-You-Want Restaurant' created at a pre-primary centre

Organising Wall Spaces

Planning of floor areas can be complemented by a 'wall view' that focuses more on display and storage spaces. Each wall can be considered as having a high space, extending roughly from the top of a teacher's raised hand to the ceiling, a middle space, from the same hand to around the waist or knees, and a low space, continuing down to floor level. Using the backs of bookshelves, doors or pianos can create more display space.

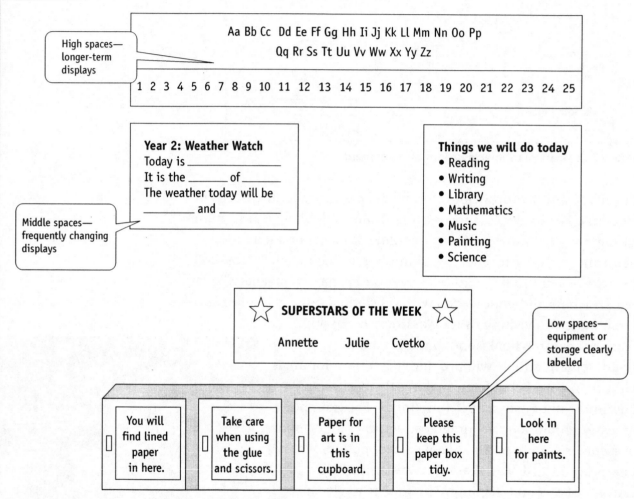

Figure 5.3: Typical use of a classroom wall

It makes sense that the high spaces are used for longer-term displays because many of these spaces are hard to reach. These spaces are also distant from the eye, so they require any lettering to be large, bold and clear. High spaces can sometimes include the ceiling, which can be used to anchor artefacts such as mobiles.

The middle spaces are suited to frequently changing displays and resources (such as books) since they are most accessible to the teacher and students. While areas for computer work and hands-on activities may have charts on display that show procedures to be followed, it is valuable to dedicate space to the representation of ongoing learning. For example, the computer area could have a flip-chart on which students can write about their discoveries.

Low spaces can't always be seen by students (except perhaps when they are seated on the floor) but, being easily accessible, are suited to storage. Having storage spaces such as cupboards, boxes, tubs, buckets and shoe-bags clearly labelled encourages students to be responsible for managing the classroom resources. Once activity areas are established it is sometimes possible to locate relevant resources nearby, resulting in smoother lesson transitions.

Ideally the bird's-eye-view plan of floor areas and the plan of wall spaces will complement each other so that the activity that occurs in an area is supported by appropriate displays and resources. For example, meeting areas are perfect places for the display of calendars and weather charts, schedules and job rosters. Meeting areas and small-group areas also need flexible display space for demonstrations of print concepts, literacy skills and activities like 'Word Sorts'. Chalkboards or whiteboards and overhead-projector screens are suitable for quick changes. Flip-charts and easels enable a permanent record to be kept. Conventional display space is useful for rearranging cards of brainstormed words into structured overviews or collaborative mind maps. Pocket charts and sentence makers can also be adapted for this purpose. Again, logistical factors will limit how compatible floor areas and wall spaces can be. The more cohesion possible, the more effective a classroom's physical environment will be.

Effective use of classroom wall space

The Classroom Culture

This section of the chapter looks at ways teachers can create and enhance the teaching and learning environment for their students with a focus on the development of a constructive classroom culture.

Nurturing a constructive classroom culture is critical to the success of every teaching and learning endeavour. The way teachers and students interact with one another is a pervasive and powerful force that has the capacity to motivate or marginalise students. Although attempts can be made to define classroom culture, its essence lies in how understandings about appropriate behaviour are enacted. Rapport, empathy and sincerity between students have their origins in values and attitudes. While teachers can model these qualities, the nurturing of a constructive classroom is unlike the logistical planning associated with arranging the physical environment. It is an ongoing response to the developmental, individual and cultural behaviours of students. Reflective teachers pick up on the tone and nature of student comments in their classroom. They think about why students are misbehaving, how a student has reacted to feedback, and whether students have become bored with lesson content or duration. This ongoing reflection, combined with a commitment to an active, purposeful learning program, is the foundation of a constructive classroom.

There are several cornerstones to creating a constructive classroom culture:
- Recognising and Celebrating Individual Difference
- Clarifying and Supporting Expectations
- Maintaining a Core of Routines
- Negotiating Aspects of the Classroom.

Recognising and Celebrating Individual Difference

There is no message of greater importance to a teacher than 'Know thy students'. By being aware of a student's individual characteristics, developmental abilities and cultural background, a teacher is able to build rapport through conversation, understand student anxieties and anticipate social and academic difficulties. It is not always necessary to implement formal measures to build knowledge about students. Much information will accumulate through conversations with the students themselves, and through similar conversations with parents, fellow teachers and the students' siblings. Often previous reports will indicate grades and achievements, attitudes and sometimes specialist diagnostic information. All of this information needs to be considered in the light of personal interactions with a student, which will help build an awareness, rather than label the student.

The following ideas can help build that awareness of a student's individual characteristics, developmental abilities and cultural background.

- Ask students to confidentially record the two classmates they would prefer to sit near. Use the data to produce a sociogram of friendships in the classroom. The analysis of the sociogram can assist teachers to make decisions about seating arrangements. Discuss the need for seating plans to be flexible and conducive to a positive learning atmosphere. Ensure that students get the opportunity to work with and be seated near a variety of peers. Seating arrangements should be altered on a regular basis.
- Observe or survey students to discover their dominant learning styles. Informal observation will often reveal students' strengths and weaknesses in visual, auditory, kinaesthetic, interactive or print-oriented learning styles.
- Be aware of the concentration span of the majority of students. Generally a student can focus for as many minutes as their age.
- Include self-descriptive activities such as a personal poem, a coat of arms or a 'Star of the Week' poster.
- Create displays that include students' names alongside home and community achievements.
- Invite students, their family members and friends to talk or write to the class about their talents and/or fame.
- Use the *First Steps* Maps of Development to record a student's development in literacy.
- Invite students to code-switch, and create bilingual or bidialectal writing when appropriate.
- Read and use texts that reflect students' cultural backgrounds.
- Take time to interact with all students on an individual basis.
- Get to know each student as a person including his or her interests and family background.

Clarifying and Supporting Expectations

All too often, what we expect from students is exactly what we get. Clarifying and supporting expectations of work standards and behaviour is pivotal to classroom management. Teachers who communicate high expectations to students and provide the support necessary to achieve these expectations are more likely to have students with high rates of academic success and who demonstrate appropriate behaviour.

Students misbehave for many reasons, and all students will misbehave at some time. Effective teachers have strategies for preventing misbehaviour and responding to it when it happens.

Students are less likely to misbehave if they:
• feel valued and respected
• have a sense of belonging
• are involved in purposeful and challenging learning experiences at an appropriate level
• see the relevance of their learning to life outside of school
• feel empowered
• know their boundaries
• know what is negotiable and what is non-negotiable.

Teachers clarify and support their expectations of behaviour in several ways. Perhaps the most obvious is through personal relationships. Teachers who develop strong personal relationships with students communicate to students that they are respected and valued as individuals. Effective teachers look for students' strengths and weaknesses rather than attaching a label. These teachers create an environment where students have a sense of belonging. Teachers can support the sense of 'belonging' by demonstrating an interest in students' personal lives and by ensuring that classroom culture encompasses all students and encourages positive interactions.

The way teachers and schools structure and organise learning communicates their expectations to students. The following questions may serve as a stimulus for reflecting on the way learning is structured and organised in the school or class.
• Is a rich and varied curriculum provided to cater for academic, personal and creative areas?
• Is the level of difficulty appropriate for students?
• Is multicultural content encouraged?
• Is the cultural background of students acknowledged and celebrated?
• Is the context of the teaching making sense to students?
• Are different learning styles and multiple intelligences being catered for?
• Are critical thinking and inquiry encouraged?
• Are questions framed to elicit higher-order responses?
• Are collaboration and cooperation encouraged?
• How are students grouped?
• Do students have the opportunity to work with a variety of other students of differing ability, social, age or cultural groups?

• Do evaluation practices promote reflection, critical thinking and problem-solving?

Finally, effective teachers communicate expectations by motivating students and encouraging them to take responsibility for their learning and behaviour. These teachers are more likely to engage students in activities that connect to their interests and strengths, and build from where they are. In this way they are fostering intrinsic motivation. They also encourage students to participate in decision-making processes in the classroom and the school to build responsibility and ownership of learning.

Maintaining a Core of Routines

Key aspects of a supportive classroom environment are stability and predictability. Routines can range from having typical times for certain activities to using the same procedures for moving into groups, yet these routines serve the purpose of providing students with social cues and expectations about how things are done. Routines are supported by physical features such as the logical location and storage of resources in clearly marked containers, shelves or cupboards, and regular reminders about accepted procedures. Where problems arise, class meetings provide a forum to solve the problem collectively by brainstorming solutions and trying out preferred options.

Most classrooms have routines for:
• entering and leaving the classroom
• beginning and concluding the day
• preparing for and returning from breaks
• moving into pairs or groups
• contributing to group discussions
• using and cleaning up resources
• handing in work
• handing out work
• moving to other classrooms or other parts of the school
• beginning regular activities such as USSR (Uninterrupted Sustained Silent Reading) or physical education
• finishing tasks
• participating in whole-school gatherings
• emergency procedures.

Where a routine is being taught or is unlikely to be remembered it makes sense to have students help to generate a routine chart. For example, students could brainstorm all the things they need to do before they enter the room at the start of the day, and write these on a large chart to be displayed just outside the classroom door. By regularly referring to the chart and questioning students about it, it is likely that they will understand, value and follow the routine.

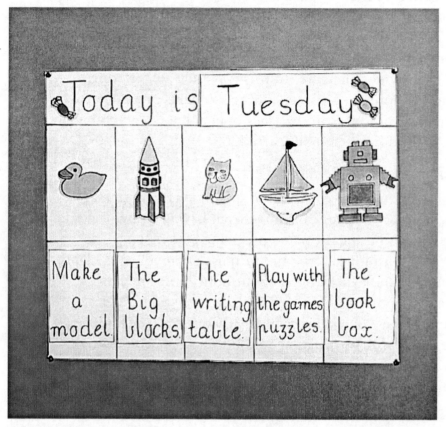

A classroom routine chart

Negotiating Aspects of the Classroom

Negotiating aspects of the curriculum, such as topics of study, and processes of classroom management such as rules, roles and responsibilities, provides students with a sense of ownership and the opportunity to share in the decision-making processes and construction of knowledge. However strong the desire to negotiate aspects of the classroom with students, there will always remain some aspects the teacher considers to be non-negotiable. Teachers should decide which aspects of the classroom can be negotiated and which should remain under their control.

When students are involved in the negotiating process, engagement, exploration and reflection are promoted. Most teachers throughout the world are required to follow a curriculum and work towards a set of desired outcomes. They are also expected to maintain standards of acceptable behaviour often set at the school level. However, within these constraints there is room to negotiate.

Negotiating 'When'

Many teachers are expected to cover certain required content in the course of the year. This may take the form of broad topics of study or lists of specific objectives. Whatever the form of the content, students can be given some choice in when they will study it. The teacher and students can negotiate:

- the order in which the topics will be covered
- when certain activities are to be completed; for example, the teacher may organise a series of activities to be completed over a period of time, and the students choose which to tackle first, second, and so on.

Negotiating 'What'

For those teachers whose curriculum provides specific topics of study, such as 'magnets' as a focus for science, there is still scope to negotiate with students. (See Figure 5.4 on page 82.)

Four questions can assist the teacher and students in focusing on the problem, question or topic to be studied.

- What do we already know about magnets?
- What do we want and need to find out about magnets?
- How will we go about finding out?
- How will we assess our accomplishments when we have finished?

Negotiation of this type helps teachers determine where students 'are at', thereby fostering learning that builds from students' existing knowledge and ideas. It acknowledges that students already possess a certain amount of knowledge about the topic and can save time by not covering aspects students already know.

Teachers can also negotiate with students the rules, roles and responsibilities that will govern their working relationship in the classroom. Students can be asked to brainstorm possible rules for inclusion as class rules and then be given the opportunity to discuss the merits of each before finally coming up with an agreed class list. Negotiated rules work well when:

- they are few in number — a maximum of five
- a rationale for each rule is discussed — explain why the rule is necessary
- ambiguous terms are explained — discuss the meaning of the words used in the rules; for example, talk about what the terms 'quiet', 'putting your hand up' or 'showing respect' mean in the context of the classroom
- the rules are stated positively — 'Raise your hand if you need something' rather than 'Don't call out.'

YEAR 1's NEGOTIATED SCIENCE PLAN: TERM 4
What We All Decided

MAGNETISM

WHAT WE ALREADY KNOW
• There are lots of different-shaped magnets.
• Magnets pick up some things and not others.
• You can do tricks with magnets.

WHAT WE WANT TO FIND OUT
• What kind of magnets do we have in our home?
• Are some magnets stronger than others?
• Do magnets pick up all metal objects?
• What does *attract* mean?
• What does *repel* mean?

ORDER OF OUR TOPICS
WEEK 1 What do magnets attract?
WEEK 2 Which magnet is stronger?
WEEK 3 Different types of magnets
WEEK 4 Magnetic force will go through things
WEEK 5 Magnetic poles

INVESTIGATION GROUPS
People we've chosen to work with:
Group 1: Maryanne, Denise, Mark, Peda, Suzi
Group 2: Tamara, Russell, Alexis, Sam, Freda
Group 3: Feni, Cvetko, Arnah, Millie, Rosco
Group 4: Mitchell, Chantelle, Tara, Heather, Brendon
Group 5: Sean, Lillico, Brooke, Danny, Matthew
Group 6: Elisha, Nathan, Warren, Marie, Blair

END-OF-TOPIC PRESENTATIONS
Show us what you have learned about magnets through one of these:

Demonstration and Oral Presentation

Audio Tape

Make a Model

Chart with Drawings

Figure 5.4: Sample negotiated science plan created by a Year 1 class

Using class meetings to negotiate plans for the organisation of the physical environment, such as use of floor areas and wall spaces, sends strong messages about the shared responsibility for managing the classroom. This negotiation and collaboration is ongoing.

Negotiating 'How'

Once the topics have been chosen and the investigation begun, the teacher and students can negotiate about how the learning will be represented when it is completed. Students will need experience of representing learning in different ways before being asked to choose for themselves. They could:

• produce a book
• make a video clip
• complete a PowerPoint presentation
• record an audio tape in conjunction with an illustrated text
• create a poster or chart
• build a model
• devise a board game.

Students can also be involved in establishing the criteria upon which judgements will be made about their representations.

For example, students may have been working together to design a PowerPoint presentation. The teacher and students can negotiate which aspects of the project are to be assessed and the degree of excellence required.

Assessment of Our PowerPoint Presentations					
		Mark Awarded			
		4	**3**	**2**	**1**
Aspects Assessed	Graphics	Graphics are related to the theme and avoid stereotypical images.	Graphics are related to the theme but include some stereotypical images.	Graphics are related to the theme but include many stereotypical images.	Graphics do not appear to be related to the theme.
	Spelling and Grammar	There are no spelling or grammatical errors in the edited version of the presentation.	There are a few (1–3) errors in spelling and grammar in the edited version of the presentation.	There are some (4–5) errors in spelling and grammar in the edited version of the presentation.	There are many errors in spelling and grammar in the edited version of the presentation.
	Sound				
	Content				
	Layout				
	Navigation				

Figure 5.5: Sample of a Negotiated Assessment Rubric

Negotiating 'With Whom'

Teachers can negotiate with students whether they will work as individuals, in pairs or in small groups. Whatever the grouping, a clear expectation about the divisions of labour need to be established before work begins. This discussion could include who will perform each task, the responsibilities of the individual group members and the consequences for those who fail to meet their responsibilities.

Classrooms need to be set up so that students are able to develop socially, academically and emotionally. When positive classroom environments have been established there is more likelihood that students will gain the necessary skills to become thoughtful, contributing members of the wider community. When implementing *First Steps* it is important that teachers establish a positive teaching and learning environment where individuals are valued, the curriculum is appropriate to the needs and strengths of students, and effective teaching and learning practices are implemented.

Students choose whether to work alone, in pairs or in small groups.

CHAPTER 6

Assessment and Evaluation: Theory, Principles and Practices

Definitions

Effective teaching and learning stems from effective assessment and evaluation. Teachers who focus on data collection as a source of valuable information to enhance learning can be successful in supporting a range of students in one classroom. In order to do this effectively classroom assessment practices need to be valid, educative, explicit, fair and comprehensive.

• Valid

The assessment needs to happen in real and meaningful contexts and to be actually assessing the particular outcomes chosen.

• Educative

The assessment needs to be educationally sound and the student should learn from the experience; e.g. the teacher provides feedback on a specific aspect so the student can concentrate on improving in that area.

• Explicit

The assessment criteria are stated clearly so the student knows what information is being gathered; e.g. tell the student that you will be questioning them about the reading strategies they were using.

• Fair

The assessment used should enable each student to demonstrate the outcomes, using their particular strengths; e.g. visual learners may choose to draw diagrams while print-oriented learners may choose to write.

• Comprehensive

A range of information should be collected in different situations over time. This may include information from observations, student products and conversations.

The terms 'assessment' and 'evaluation' are often used synonymously, but are in fact separate stages in the process of teaching and learning. There is a simple distinction between the two.

Assessment refers to the stage of gathering data. Effective teachers gather and record information constantly in a range of ways — through observation, conversations and student products.

Evaluation is the stage of making judgements about the information gathered, when the teacher draws conclusions about the progress of students and the effectiveness of teaching plans. There are two broad types of evaluation. Formative evaluation occurs during the learning activity or unit of work and is aimed at improving the learning experiences and student outcomes along the way. Summative evaluation occurs at the end of the learning activity or unit of work and focuses on the effectiveness of the learning experience and student outcomes.

The analysis of data is essential because assessment without evaluation is meaningless. Figure 6.1 illustrates the meaningful combination of the assessment (data gathering) and evaluation (drawing conclusions) processes.

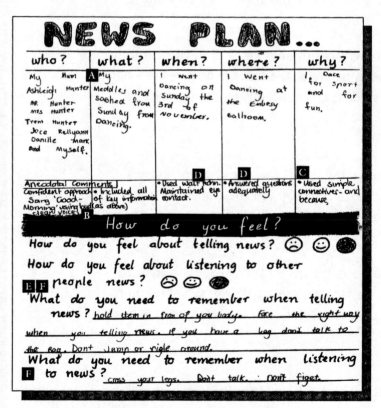

Assessment process includes data-gathering in the form of:
- Sample of work: News Plan
- Observation during oral recount: recorded as anecdotal notes by teacher
- Self-evaluation: comments from student, included in work sample

Evaluative comments made from assessment
A Describes real events in logical sequence and includes key information in recount event.
B Considers occasions when voice volume is adjusted according to purpose and situation.
C Uses connectives.
D Attends to responses of others and elaborates.
E Reflects on own speaking and listening.
F Applies techniques introduced.

Education Department of Western Australia 1998,
Outcomes and Standards Framework: Work Samples

Figure 6.1: Assessment and evaluation

Successful Assessment and Evaluation

Effective teachers:
- have a **clear purpose** for all assessment and evaluation processes used
- collect information in an **ongoing** way in a range of **authentic contexts**
- use a **wide range** of appropriate **tools and methods** to gather information
- use a **collaborative approach** to collect information about students
- create systems to **record** and **manage** data
- **make adaptations** to assessment and evaluation processes when necessary
- take time to **analyse** and **evaluate** the information gathered and make judgements about future teaching.

Clear Purpose

Although there is a range of reasons for conducting literacy assessment in classrooms, the prime purpose needs to be to provide teachers with information that will help plan relevant and meaningful literacy instruction. This supports the view that teaching is an ongoing process of reflection and that curriculum decisions are driven primarily by students' needs. Valuable time spent on data collection must provide teachers with information that will enhance learning in classrooms.

Assessment can be used to:
- determine students' interests, strengths and phases of literacy development
- inform decisions about how best to support students' literacy development
- monitor student development
- provide a tool for reflecting on and improving teaching
- provide information about students that can be shared with others.

Ongoing Assessment in Authentic Contexts

The most valuable type of assessment information is collected on a continuing basis. Assessment and evaluation should not be something that happens only at the beginning and end of a topic, semester or school year. The process of collecting data about individuals, small groups or whole classes of students can be incorporated into a regular school day. Powerful assessment takes place when teachers observe students at work during regular classroom activities. Information gathered on an ongoing basis, while students interact with learning experiences that are part of the regular classroom plan, provides teachers with useful data from a range of contexts. Consider the multitude of classroom events that may provide authentic contexts for the collection of data about literacy development. These could include shared, modelled and guided literacy sessions, retellings, drama, poetry reading, readers' theatre, reading response activities, library visits, independent reading time and literacy events across the content areas. Essentially every learning experience will reveal something about a student's performance. Assessment is largely the art of knowing what to record, when, why and how.

Range of Tools and Methods

It is important that teachers develop a repertoire of tools and methods for collecting data about students' literacy development. A balance of observation, conversation and analysis of products is essential. This multifaceted approach to assessment, including a range of tools, can assist teachers to determine which methods of data collection are providing the best information.

Collaborative Approach

A collaborative approach to assessment involves and values the input from a range of sources including the student, parents or caregivers, peers and teachers.

Parents and caregivers are a rich source of information and often provide unique insights into the literacy development of their children. Involving parents in the assessment of students' literacy development can provide an additional dimension to the data collection process in any classroom. It is critical that classroom teachers value parent input and encourage them to share information in both formal and informal ways. A variety of suggestions about how teachers have involved parents and caregivers in the assessment process (including sample formats) are provided within this chapter.

Given time and support, students of all ages are also capable of providing worthwhile insights into their own literacy development. There are many ways of encouraging students to be part of the assessment and evaluation process. Learning journals, logs, work samples and surveys are examples of useful tools that can be used.

Systems to Record and Manage Data

Gathering and recording information about many students at one time can often be overwhelming and unclear. Many teachers design innovative processes and formats in an attempt to make the process more systematic and manageable. The *First Steps* Maps of Development provide a framework to assist teachers to record and manage the data collected about individuals or groups of students. The Maps of Development are not a data-collection tool within themselves, but are an excellent framework for recording and making sense of an array of information. Placing students on the Maps allows teachers to compile information and create a common language across a school to identify the development of each student and discuss with others. Once information is recorded these maps assist teachers to make informed decisions about the future teaching and learning needs of students.

Teachers also design innovative ways of storing *First Steps* Individual Profile sheets.

- Hanging folders in a filing cabinet are sometimes created for each student.
- A large A3-sized file is often used to store all profiles in one place.
- Profile sheets are sometimes attached inside individual student portfolios.

Adaptations

Teachers need the flexibility to use a range of data-assessment tools across the one classroom. The tools selected will depend on the changing needs of the student population. It may be necessary to collect more information about students who appear to have special needs. More detailed information about these particular students will help teachers focus on how best to support their development. It is not imperative that teachers use the same forms of assessment for each student if the ongoing focus is on fairness, validity, comprehensiveness and instructional planning.

Analysis of Information

Effective teachers take time to analyse any information gathered about students' literacy development and use it to make judgements about future teaching. Simply collecting and then recording information about literacy development does not necessarily mean the data is providing the teacher with anything useful. Most information collected still requires some form of analysis to clarify its meaning and possible implications.

Analysing information enables teachers to identify strengths and needs, look for patterns or discrepancies, identify developmental phases and, most importantly, to design learning plans. This is often a challenging task for teachers. The *First Steps* Maps of Development assist teachers with both the analysis and the planning of appropriate learning experiences for the whole class, small groups or individual students. The use of indicators and phases will highlight strengths of individual students and significant developmental signposts that have been reached. The Major Teaching Emphases at each phase will support the process of selecting appropriate future learning experiences. Major Teaching Emphases linked to each phase of development have been created to support where students are, to challenge their current level of development and to support identified needs.

A Process for Assessment and Evaluation

Figure 6.2 represents a process for planning and implementing effective assessment and evaluation. It also suggests a way of incorporating the use of the *First Steps* Maps of Development. Focus questions provide a framework for decisions that may need to be made. These include:

- What information is needed?
- What are the most efficient and valid ways to collect the information and from whom?
- How can the information be collected?
- How can the information be recorded?
- What can be done with the information?
- How can the information be shared with others?

The remainder of this chapter will support teachers in answering these types of questions in an informed and open way. Ideas for reporting and sharing information with others are also included. Further information specific to Reading, Writing, Speaking and Listening, and Viewing can be found in the Map of Development book for each strand.

A Process for Assessment and Evaluation

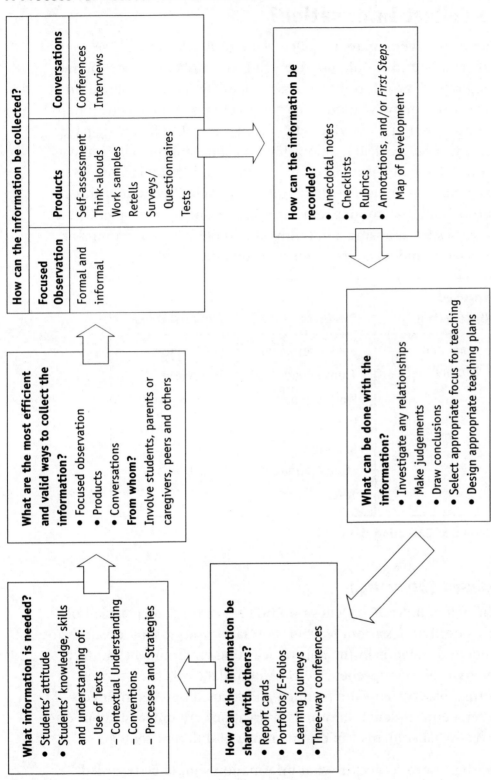

How can the information be collected?

Focused Observation	Products	Conversations
Formal and informal	Self-assessment Think-alouds Work samples Retells Surveys/ Questionnaires Tests	Conferences Interviews

How can the information be recorded?
- Anecdotal notes
- Checklists
- Rubrics
- Annotations, and/or *First Steps* Map of Development

What are the most efficient and valid ways to collect the information?
- Focused observation
- Products
- Conversations

From whom?
Involve students, parents or caregivers, peers and others

What can be done with the information?
- Investigate any relationships
- Make judgements
- Draw conclusions
- Select appropriate focus for teaching
- Design appropriate teaching plans

What information is needed?
- Students' attitude
- Students' knowledge, skills and understanding of:
  – Use of Texts
  – Contextual Understanding
  – Conventions
  – Processes and Strategies

How can the information be shared with others?
- Report cards
- Portfolios/E-folios
- Learning journeys
- Three-way conferences

Figure 6.2

What Are the Most Efficient and Valid Ways to Collect Information?

There are several ways to collect data in the classroom. The way data is collected should provide valid, educative, explicit, fair and comprehensive information. Assessment can be 'streamlined' in the classroom by 'working smarter' to eliminate time-consuming methods that may provide little information. The following pages provide a range of suggestions for collecting information in the form of focused observation, products or conversations. All examples can be used across multiple literacy experiences and as part of daily classroom events. It is important to develop efficient processes for assessing and to involve students, peers, parents or caregivers, and teachers when collecting data.

Focused Observation	Products	Conversations
Formal and informal	Self-assessment Think-alouds Work samples Retells Surveys/ Questionnaires Tests	Conferences Interviews

Figure 6.3: Collecting data

Focused Observation

The ability to STOP, LOOK and LISTEN is a fundamental skill of any effective classroom teacher. Formal or informal observations of student behaviour in the natural learning environment can form the basis of a comprehensive classroom data-collection process. Formal observations are planned and focus on predetermined criteria and students. Informal observations are unplanned but often reveal what students can do in a range of different contexts.

Teachers need to decide what information should be recorded during formal or informal observations. Initially, anything that seems significant is acceptable. However, if observational records are going to be useful at a later date, it is critical that teachers become skilled in knowing exactly what to look for. Focused observation is more powerful than observation alone. The *First Steps* Maps of

Development provide teachers with the necessary support to help focus their observations on significant behaviours related to literacy development.

Focused observation encompasses not only knowing what to look for, but also concentrating on one student or particular students at any one time. It is impossible for classroom teachers to observe and record information about all students, every day. By selecting five or six students to focus on over a short period of time, such as a day or a week, each child is observed systematically throughout the course of a month, semester or year.

Developing high quality observation skills takes time and practice. An excellent model developed by many schools implementing *First Steps* is to organise 'observation buddies' or pairs of teachers to support each other in the observation process. It is an ideal opportunity to closely observe students when another teacher is taking responsibility for teaching the class. This frees the observer to watch and listen to students and to gain a deeper understanding of the processes and strategies being used.

Products

The assessment of both process and product is important when making decisions about supporting students' literacy development. As well as using focused observation for assessment in a classroom, teachers also need to consider what further information can be gathered from students' oral, written or visual work products. Teachers can assess student products that have been created during the process of learning, not only the final products that are a result of learning. For example, it is just as important to collect planning sheets and draft writing samples as it is to collect published writing products. The *First Steps* Maps of Development provide teachers with the necessary support to analyse selected work products.

Observation and analysis of students' products such as self-assessment forms, think-alouds, work samples (including multi-media creations), retells, surveys or questionnaires, and tests all provide insights into literacy development.

1 Self-assessment Products

Student self-assessment is a critical part of developing a student's responsibility for his or her own learning. Self-assessment procedures can also provide teachers with insights into the student's literacy development that otherwise may not be apparent. It is critical that formats are modelled and provided for students as a framework for recording information and reflections. With teacher support and guidance, students can develop the skills necessary to assess their own learning. There is a variety of tools that can be used to encourage students to reflect on and make judgements about their learning. These include student logs, goal-setting frameworks and journals.

• Log Formats

The simplest form of self-assessment is the student's log to record work completed.

RECORD OF BOOKS READ — SEMESTER ONE		
DATE STARTED	**TEXT TITLE**	**DATE FINISHED**
Mon 10 Feb	Unreal – Paul Jennings	Tues 18 Feb
Thurs 20 Feb	Journey – Patricia MacLachlan	Mon 24 Feb
Wed 26 Feb	Undone – Paul Jennings	Mon 3 March

Figure 6.4: Simple student log

Logs can be extended to reveal individual interests, preferences, attitudes or understandings. Students are not only asked to record completed work but also to reflect on some aspect of the task.

My Reading Log

Title: Land slide

Author: Colin Thiele

I chose this book....
because I like chapter books.

I thought that....
it was excellent and it gives a look at what it would be like in another state.

I want to read...
Seacaves by Colin Thiele.

Kasey-Rose   Age :9

Figure 6.5: Reading log sample

My Writing Log

Date: 16/09/02   Name: Jaye

Date Completed: 20ᵗʰ August

Title: (Shul) Should Children Do Homework?

Form: Exposition

Comment: I could have gone a bit better with my grammar my point s were clear I was persuading children to do homework.

Date: 13/09/02

Date Completed: 29ᵗʰ August

Title: How Does a Bike Move?

Form: Explanation

Comment: I think I might have left out some of it in parts. Put more detail in.

Figure 6.6: Writing log sample

Viewing Log

Name: Helayna

Title	My Purpose For Viewing	Producer/s' Purpose	General Comment
"Home And Away"	Because it's my favourite show.	So people will like the show.	There was a sad bit when the Dad said "Lets go on a picnic" to the Mum.
"The Great Outdoors"	I like to see where the people go.	To let people know about other places in the world.	i like the people on there.
"Brum"	Because I like cars.	Because they might have liked cars.	Brum has eyes, they make him look funny.
"The Mermaid Princess"	Because I like fairies.	The Author likes fairies.	I liked all the colourful pictures in the book.

Figure 6.7: Viewing log sample

MY WRITING LOG									
Purpose	Audience	Form	Subject	Plan	Draft	Revise and Edit	Conference	Proofread	Publish
I want to …	Who?	So I'm writing a …	About …						
Entertain	Pre-P Kids	Poem	Space	31/3	31/3	4/4			

Figure 6.8: Writing log sample

• Other Formats

It is also important to encourage students to reflect on their own learning processes and strategies, personal strengths and areas for improvement. A multitude of commercially produced formats are available in all areas of literacy. Teachers use such formats as a basis for adaptation to meet their own students' particular needs. This ensures that the formats are directly related to the context of the classroom and students.

Sample Formats for Reflection

Student Self-Assessment
Transitional Reading Phase

Name: _____   Date: _____

First Steps: Look What I Can Do

My Reading Behaviours—I can:	Not Yet	Sometimes	Consistently
• State the main idea of a text and provide details from the text to support it			
• Discuss information that is stated in a text			
• Select information from a text for a specific purpose			
• Link ideas both stated and implied; e.g. tell about cause and effect			
• Use the library system and search engines to locate and select suitable texts for a specific purpose			
• Check the currency and relevance of information for a specific purpose			
• Tell when authors are trying to make me think about something their way			
• Tell why my interpretation of a text may be different from someone else's			
• Recognise devices that authors and illustrators use to construct meaning; e.g. word selection, visuals			
• Challenge and discuss author's choice of content in a text; e.g. validity, accuracy, credibility			
• Speculate on the reasons why an author chose to represent a character/person a certain way			
• Recognise a bank of words in different places, including less common words and subject specific words			
• Know some different sounds for the same letter combinations; e.g. rough, dough, plough			
• Self correct if I make a mistake			
• Use strategies—such as reading on, re-reading and using syllables—to work out words I don't know			
• Use my knowledge of text form, purpose, structure, organisation and language features to assist when reading and completing tasks			
• Use punctuation effectively to enhance comprehension and oral reading			
• Use a range of strategies to maintain, monitor and adjust my comprehension; e.g. creating images, determining importance			
• Think of things I already know about a topic when I'm reading a text			
• Re-read if I lose meaning			
Things I enjoy:			
• Listen to a variety of texts			
• Read for pleasure			
• Read favourite texts and authors as well as discovering new ones			
• Read to learn about things			
• Discuss and compare texts			

Figure 6.9: Look What I Can Do—Transitional reading phase

> **Self-assessment Sheet:**
> **Comprehension Strategies**
>
> Name _Jaye Age 8_
>
> Did you have any problems understanding
> while reading this text? _No, I didn't_
>
> How did you solve the problem? _____
> _____
>
> What strategies did you use while reading?
> _word understanding_
> _reading fluently in my head_
>
> Are there other strategies that may also have
> worked with this text? _No_

Figure 6.10: Structured format

'Two Stars and a Wish' provides students with a simple framework for reflecting on positive aspects of their work as well as focusing on areas for improvement. It also provides a simple framework for peer assessment.

> Two stars = things I can do or things I'm good at
> Wish = something I need to work on
>
> Two Stars and a Wish for _Jemma_ Age 9
>
> ☆ _understand what I_
> _read_
>
> ☆ _read quickly_
>
> _If I get stuck_
> _on a word's meaning_
> _ask someone about it_

Figure 6.11: 'Two Stars and a Wish' sample

• Goal-setting Frameworks

Personal goal-setting is another form of self-assessment suitable for all ages. Before students can independently create learning goals it is essential for teachers to provide ongoing modelling and scaffolding. Helping students to identify achievable goals that are linked to personal and shared targets promotes a sense of ownership. Goal-setting frameworks can provide a focus for beginning goal-setting in the classroom.

Me as A Reader

🙂

Name: *Lina*   Age: 9

The kinds of reading I like to do are:
Adventure and Mystery

I like reading when:
I'm in bed at night

I am getting better at:
reading with expresion

Now I want to get better at:
reading fluently

✐ Writing Goals for Term 2

1. _____

2. _____

3. _____

4. _____

Figures 6.12a and b: Frameworks for goal-setting

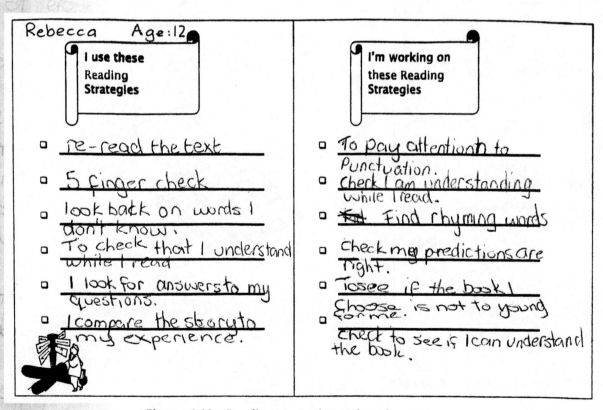

Rebecca   Age: 12

I use these Reading Strategies

- re-read the text
- 5 finger check
- look back on words I don't know.
- To check that I understand while I read
- I look for answers to my questions.
- I compare the story to my experience.

I'm working on these Reading Strategies

- To pay attention to Punctuation.
- Check I am understanding while I read.
- Find rhyming words
- Check my predictions are right.
- To see if the book I choose is not to young for me.
- Check to see if I can understand the book.

Figure 6.12c: Reading strategies and goals

• Journals

Journals also provide an opportunity for students to reflect on their own learning. The process of inviting students to reflect and write about an aspect of their literacy can provide further information and insights into individual development. A written conversation between teacher and student may also occur as a result of the journal entries. Young students who are unable to write responses can use drawing or be involved in keeping a class journal.

Journals can take many forms, each providing a different focus for reflection. The purpose and desired outcomes of using a journal in the classroom can direct the type of journal used. A range of journals have been successfully used, including:

– Reading Response Journals
A simple record of thoughts and questions about the texts students are reading. Adhesive notes make an excellent tool for students to record these thoughts as they read.

– Dialogue Journals
A 'conversation' in writing conducted with a peer or teacher. A student writes a response or question about a text and the teacher or peer writes a short response back.

– Reflective Journals
Have a focus on particular literacy activities reflecting on the process, feelings and outcomes of the event.

– Metacognitive Journals
Encourage students to think about and become aware of their own thought processes when constructing and comprehending texts. 'What have I learned?' and 'How did I learn it?' are two key questions for students to consider.

– Summative Journals
May be completed at the end of a theme, unit of work or period of time. Students reflect on a series of past literacy events and consider future application of new learning.

Journal Scaffolds

Reading Response Journal Sentence Starters

I began to think of ...
I love the way ...
I can't believe ...
I wonder why ...
I noticed ...
I think ...
If I were ...
I'm not sure ...
My favourite character is ...
I like the way the author ...
I felt sad when ...
I wish that ...
This reminds me of ...

Figure 6.13: Reading journal

Dialogue Journal

Student:
I read "Koala Lou" by Mem Fox. I read it to myself but I wanted to read it aloud because I loved the sound of the words. I felt the story was about me because I never come first at anything.

Teacher:
I love the sound of words too. Remember, winning isn't everything! I like you just the way you are.

Figure 6.14: Sample entries

_____'s Reflective Journal		
Event 1	Feelings	Learning
Event 2	Feelings	Learning
Event 3	Feelings	Learning

Figure 6.15: Reflective journal framework

Learning How to Learn in Writing

Choose a piece of writing you have recently completed.

Record the steps you took to complete this piece.

Share your process with a friend, explaining exactly what you did.

Figure 6.16: Metacognitive journal framework

Thinking About Your Writing

Name: Alex   Age: 9   Date: 05.08.02.

1. I found this piece of writing (Easy) Difficult (circle one)

2. The best part of this piece of writing is The letter but i had a few spelling mistakes.

I did this by I did this with some help and talking to other people.

3. Something I want to work on for the future is Not getting so many spelling mistakes.

I plan to do this by Practicing my spelling at school and home.

Thinking About Your Writing

Name: Louise   (Age 10)   Date: 19.9.02

1. I found this piece of writing (Easy) Difficult (circle one)

2. The best part of this piece of writing is the planning because you can organise who did what and where and things like that.

I did this by watching the teacher model doing the plan a couple of times

3. Something I want to work on for the future is using more descriptive language

I plan to do this by thinking about how the character did or said something.

Thinking About Your Writing

Name: RebeccaLynn   Age: 12   Date: 18-9-02

1. I found this piece of writing (Easy) Difficult (circle one)

2. The best part of this piece of writing is it was very detailed.

I did this by adding adjectives and verbs

3. Something I want to work on for the future is To structure my writing correctly so it is easy to read.

I plan to do this by looking at class charts and taking my time.

Figures 6.17a, b and c: Metacognitive journal samples

2 Think-alouds

Think-alouds are articulations of thoughts before, during and after literacy events. They may be spontaneous reactions to the text by students or may be encouraged or requested by the teacher. The analysis of think-alouds can provide a rich source of information about literacy processes and strategies being used.

In the example that follows, the teacher has asked a student to record their think-aloud on an adhesive note and highlight the particular reference in the text. The students have been taught to code the strategies they are using (T-S is a text-to-self connection, FU-S is employing a fix-up strategy). See the Reading Resource Book for further information about these strategies.

T-S

Before I even started reading I saw the title and it reminded me of Naime's story!

The Monster Fish by Colin Thiele

Ben lived by the sea. He loved fishing and often went out in the boat with his mum and dad. Once a year the Big Boomer fishing contest was held. There was a prize for the person who caught the biggest fish on a hand line.

Ben was checking his fishing tackle for the contest when the phone rang. His mum answered it. 'Your cousin Andy is on his way,' she told Ben. 'He wants to come fishing with us.' Ben's dad rolled his eyes. 'That boy is as clumsy as a puppy,' he said. 'He's sure to fall out of the boat.' 'He'll be OK,' Mum said. 'He'll catch something.' Dad snorted. 'The only thing he'll catch is a cold.'

FU-S

I re-read the bit where it said 'He wants to go fishing with us.'

Figure 6.18: Student think-aloud notes

3 Work Samples

A work sample is anything completed by students in authentic literacy situations from which judgements about literacy development can be made. Work samples can be oral, written or visual. They provide teachers with valuable information about students' development. It is important to collect a range of work samples from different contexts before making definitive judgements about student progress. These samples may include comprehension activities, writing samples, models, pictures and diagrams, oral presentations, PowerPoint presentations, research projects and cross-curriculum tasks.

Teachers need to be aware of the learning situation in which the samples were created. Consideration of the level of support provided, the processes and strategies used by the individual student and the group dynamics involved may all influence the outcome of the product being assessed. Samples can be dated and annotated to highlight the specific learning that has taken place, or that needs to happen. These samples can be selected for inclusion in portfolios, or used as a basis for discussion with students and/or parents to illustrate student achievement.

4 Retells

Asking students to retell oral, visual or written texts provides an excellent opportunity for teachers to gather information about a variety of aspects of literacy development; e.g. comprehension, grammar, spelling, speaking, text structure.

Retelling is a simple activity that is flexible in its use and provides an opportunity for students to transform a text into their own words after reading, listening or viewing. The retelling procedure requires students to read, or listen to a text, organise key information they have understood from the text and then prepare to share and compare their retell with others. Retells can be shared orally, in a written form, as a drawing or through drama.

The assessment of student retells will be determined by the focus area the teacher has chosen. Some may choose to focus on text structure or sequence; others may look specifically at the language used or the overall comprehension of the text. Recording sheets can be created to focus the observations on the chosen areas. The following example illustrates a recording sheet created to focus specifically on organisation and content of the retell.

RETELLING RECORD SHEET Name _____ Date _____ Text chosen _____		well developed	partial	not evident
Orientation **Setting**	Tells where the story happens Tells when the story happens			
Characters	Includes all the characters Describes some character traits			
Events	All main events included Events described in order			
Details	Includes relevant details			
Comments				

Figure 6.19

5 Surveys and Questionnaires

Surveys and questionnaires typically consist of a series of statements or questions about which students or parents are asked to express their agreement, disagreement, or other response. Surveys and questionnaires can be created and customised to link to a particular assessment focus; e.g. values, interest, emotions and attitudes, confidence, or processes and products.

The Indicators from the *First Steps* Maps of Development support teachers in creating observational frameworks for parents. The following examples illustrate how surveys can be adapted to suit a particular purpose.

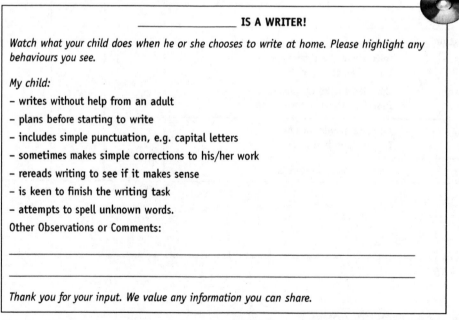

MY CHILD AS A READER

Please indicate your observations of your child's reading in the following areas:

Reading Behaviours	Comment
Jack enjoys reading at home.	Often found in bed reading late at night with his special light. Just loves his book collection. Enjoys all sorts of books. Jack enjoys a visit to the local library every Saturday morning
Jack borrows books from the local library.	
Jack likes to read a variety of books.	He spends much of his time on the computer looking at websites.
When _Jack_ comes to an unknown word she/he usually: ✓ guesses the word ✓ uses pictures to help – misses out the word – attempts to sound out the word.	Jack will always look closely at the pictures when reading and makes use of them for working out words he doesn't know. Pretty clever I think.

Figure 6.20a: Parent survey — focus on reading

_____ **IS A WRITER!**

Watch what your child does when he or she chooses to write at home. Please highlight any behaviours you see.

My child:
- writes without help from an adult
- plans before starting to write
- includes simple punctuation, e.g. capital letters
- sometimes makes simple corrections to his/her work
- rereads writing to see if it makes sense
- is keen to finish the writing task
- attempts to spell unknown words.

Other Observations or Comments:

_____

_____

Thank you for your input. We value any information you can share.

Figure 6.20b: Parent survey—focus on writing

Reading Attitude Questionnaire

Place a cross on the line that shows how you feel about reading.

1 Do you like to read books at home?

Yes, a lot ← ——————————————— → No, not at all

2 Do you like to get books for presents?

Yes, a lot ← ——————————————— → No, not at all

3 Do you like someone reading books to you?

Yes, a lot ← ——————————————— → No, not at all

4 Do you like to read in free time at school?

Yes, a lot ← ——————————————— → No, not at all

5 Do you like to read different kinds of books?

Yes, a lot ← ——————————————— → No, not at all

Figure 6.21: Student survey—focus on reading

6 Tests

Testing is another way of gathering data about a student's literacy development. It is important to remember that a single test, used in isolation, may provide a misguided sense of development. Test results are of more value when used in conjunction with other assessment tools.

There are several types of tests available including:
– Criterion-referenced Tests
– Norm-referenced Tests (often referred to as Standardised Tests)
– Teacher-made Tests.

• Criterion-referenced tests are designed to measure whether or not students have mastered certain skills, so the test will include only those items that measure the skills in question.

• Norm-referenced tests are those in which scoring, norms and administration have been established as a result of former use with a large number of students. The performances of other students on the test are presented as norms for the purpose of comparing achievement.

If teachers wish to use a criterion- or norm-referenced test to collect information about their students' literacy development, the following factors need to be considered.

- The tests may be 'normed' on populations very different from those taking the test.
- The tests may be biased against certain populations of students.
- The tests may be culturally loaded in favour of one culture over another.
- A test in English is inappropriate for a student who has little or no proficiency in the language.
- The tests may contain items that are conceptually unfamiliar to the students.
- Scores alone do not indicate why students performed the way they did or offer teachers suggestions for future directions.
- The tests may not measure what students have been taught.
- The tests may be out-of-date or out-of-step with the current group of students.

- Teacher-made tests can be created to focus on any aspect of students' literacy development that needs to be assessed. These tests can provide a clearer picture of students' literacy development because they can be tailored by the teacher to suit the purpose, audience and context.

Conversations

One of the most important ways to assess students' literacy development is through the use of talk. Unplanned brief conversations or scheduled conferences and interviews with individuals provide teachers with valuable information that may not be collected in other contexts. Teachers who ensure they are speaking to students and/or parents on a regular basis often gain a deeper understanding of the development of individual students.

1 Conferences

There is a variety of conference formats involving different audiences and groupings. These include:
- One-on-one conferences – teacher and student
- Peer conferences – student and student
- Small-group conferences – students
- Three-way conferences – student, teacher and parent.

Each of these conference situations can provide a teacher with a data-collection opportunity; however, the one-on-one teacher–student conference also provides the opportunity for individual instruction.

Effective one-on-one conferencing centres on building relationships with individual students. Open conversations elicit accurate information that will allow teachers to support each student's needs. For conferences to be successful students need to know what is expected of them. They need to know what their role is, how the conference will be structured and what records will be kept. Each student–teacher conference will take its own pathway but a framework for planning is useful.

- Identify the Focus for the Conference
  What are you working on?
  Where are you up to?
  How can I help you?

- Invite Input from the Student
  Read a text, share some writing.

- Offer Praise
  Talk about strengths.

- Ask Questions

- Suggest Future Action
  Offer suggestions.

- Closure

Role of Teacher in Teacher–Student Conferences

Select a particular focus.

Create and use a flexible format.

Introduce new strategies and processes.

Encourage the student to talk.

Provide feedback to the student.

Create a sense of partnership.

Record information after each conference.

Role of Student in Teacher–Student Conferences

Be prepared. Have materials ready and a chosen topic for discussion.

List some things that you are pleased about in your reading, writing, speaking, listening or viewing. Be willing to discuss these.

Share your previous goals. Discuss any problems you may have had with the achievement of the goal.

Be prepared to set some new goals.

Student/Teacher Conference Record Sheet	Student/Teacher Conference Record Sheet
Name: Jemma Age: 9	Name: Jordan Age: 6
Conference Date: 20/9/02	Conference Date: 17/9/02
Identified Focus: Re-reading when meaning is lost	Identified Focus: Structure of a Recount
Praise Offered: Great decoding, good fluency.	Praise Offered: Great writing because it has a title ; included who, what, when, lots of words spelt correctly ; included feelings
Discussion Questions: What to do when lose meaning? How can you become a better reader? Tell me what has happened in the story so far?	Discussion Questions: What did you find most challenging? Putting my fullstops in the right place.
Suggestions Made: To use a clearer/louder voice To stop every chapter to think about what the story is telling her	Suggestions Made: Read back over as you are writing to make sure it makes sense ; concentrate on 'b' and 'd'
Insights About Student Competent reader - decodes well, orally hard to hear comprehends well, - mostly	Insights About Student Jordan is a keen reader but his reading ability is low compared to his writing ability displayed. Is easily distracted by others but an enthusiastic participant.

Figures 6.22a and b: Conference record sheets

2 Interviews

Interviews are a one-on-one question-and-answer conversation between a teacher and student or a teacher and parent. Depending on the type of questions asked, conducting interviews can provide a wealth of useful assessment information. Interviews are most effective when conducted orally since this allows teachers to ask follow-up questions that help clarify, justify or exemplify initial responses. Written responses to interview questions are also useful, as they can be taken away and analysed at a later time.

• Interviews with Students

Interviews with students provide a prime opportunity to listen actively and encourage them to verbalise their thought processes. Planning questions that elicit rich information and encourage the students to do most of the talking is a challenge. Effective interview questions are focused, open and probing. These types of questions would encourage open and honest answers, have no single right answer and relate specifically to the type of information the teacher is seeking.

Teachers can design questions to focus on different elements including knowledge, attitude, strategies or task completion. The purpose and desired outcomes of the interview will govern the types of questions chosen. The following examples illustrate the focus on different elements.

Reading Interview Questions: Focus on Knowledge

Q: *Can you tell me what reading is?*
Peter: It's when you get a book and you read it, what's inside it.

Q: *When you read what do you do?*
Peter: I say the words out loud.

Q *Who Reads?*
Peter: The teacher, me, everybody.

Figure 6.23: Reading interview record

Writing Interview Questions: Focus on Strategies

Q: *Are you a good writer? Why?*
I think I am pretty good because sometimes I think of things and sometimes I can't, so that makes me pretty good.

Q: *What makes you a good writer? Why?*
I think my imagination makes me a good writer because my parents have very good heads too so they must have passed it on to ME.

Q: *When you are writing and you get stuck what do you do?*
I let my imagination go crazy and write what comes first in my head that makes sense.

Q: *When you don't know how to spell a word what do you do?*
If I get stuck with a word i give it a go or sound it out and then underline it so the teacher knows I can't spell it.

Q: *Who do you think is a good writer? Why?*
I think it would be the author of Harry Potter because she has really good ideas and has very good first 4 books that were out.

Q: *What do you like best about your own writing?*
I like my neatness and the way I write it and then I like to look back and be proud of it.

Luisa (Age 11)

Figure 6.24: Writing interview record

Teacher asks the questions and records the answers

Writing Interview Questions: Focus on Strategies

Q: *Are you a good writer?*
Why? I think I am a good writer because I write with a lot of detail.

Q *What makes you a good writer? Why?*
I read alot so that makes me a good writer, and I put sentences from books into my own words and put them in my writing

Q: *When you are writing and you get stuck what do you do?* I keep on thinking back to what I have written and make sense of it, and then decide what to put next.

Q: *When you don't know how to spell a word what do you do?* I normally write in my spelling journal and then go to the teacher to check it.

Q: *Who do you think is a good writer? Why?*
J. K. Rowling because she writes exciting and adventurous stories and uses good words.

Q: *What do you like best about your own writing?*
I like the way I use exciting words and I put mystery and adventure into my stories. I also write quite neatly.

Katie (Age 9)

Figure 6.25: Writing interview record

Reading Interview Questions: Focus on Attitude

Q: *What kinds of reading do you like to do?*
I like novels like Harry Potter and I like reading fiction more than Non fiction.

Q: *Who is your favourite author?*
I like Roal Dailh and J. K rowling

Q: *When do you most like to read?*
At night before I go to bed and after lunch to settle down.

Q: *How often do you read at home?*
I read every morning and night is my favourite time to read.

Q: *How do you feel when you receive a book as a gift?*
I feel like jwow!, I wonder whats this is about and if I don't like it I leave it in my shelf and forget about it

Q: *How do you feel about going to the local library or bookshop?* I don't go to the local library I just go to a book shop and buy something that sounds intering.

Q: *How do you feel about reading at school?*

Luisa (Age 11)

Figure 6.26: Reading interview record

Literacy Interview Questions: Focus on Task Completion

What are you doing?

How are you going to complete the task?

What do you hope the outcome will be?

How will you know you were successful?

Figure 6.27: Literacy interview questions

• Interviews with Parents

When conducting interviews with parents the teacher's questions can be planned to elicit information that will lead to a better understanding of the student and to more effective teaching plans.

Sample Parent–Teacher Interview Questions: Focus on Reading

What type of reading does your child like to do at home?

How often does your child choose to read at home?

How does your child feel about receiving a book as a gift?

What are your family's favourite books, authors, characters, videos and DVDs?

Does your child notice and read print in the environment?

What would you like your child to do as a reader?

What do you think your child needs to do to become a better reader?

How does your child usually respond when he or she has finished reading a book?

Figure 6.28: Parent interview questions

Note: Further information, including examples, about focused observation, products, and conversations within each strand can be found in the Maps of Development.

How Can the Information Be Recorded?

Teachers have devised a range of innovative ways to record the array of information they gather about students' literacy development. The use of computers or palm pilots often helps teachers streamline the time it takes to record information. Some ways of recording the information, on paper or electronically, include:

- Anecdotal Notes
- Checklists
- Rubrics
- Annotations
- *First Steps* Maps of Development.

1 Anecdotal Notes

When teachers record short descriptions of observations in the classroom these recordings are often done at the time of the event and are referred to as anecdotal notes. Anecdotal notes are objective factual observations and should help a teacher to recognise and interpret individual patterns of learning over time. Teachers choose to record anecdotal notes in a variety of ways including: observation grids, adhesive notes, in notebooks, on index cards, in binders divided into sections for each student, or with the help of multi-media devices. All work equally well and it is highly recommended that each teacher experiment with a variety until they discover the best possible process for them and their students. Below are some examples of how teachers have managed the recording of formal and informal observations.

• Observation Grids

Prepared observation grids allow teachers to quickly record any observations of the selected group of students. Multiple copies of the observation grid may be needed if the teacher is observing the same students over an entire week.

Teacher: _____ Class: _____		
Date: _____		
Focus: _____		
Name	Name	Name
Name	Name	Name

Figure 6.29: Observation grid

• Adhesive Notes

Adhesive notes (Post-It Notes™, Marbig Notes™, Stikki Notes™)
are small, can be tucked inside a pocket and are a versatile resource
for recording anecdotal information. Notes about the selected
students can be sorted at the end of the day and attached to an
individual's folder, book or card. Computer label stickers are also
an innovative alternative to adhesive notes.

AP Spent entire SSR time with big book from shared-reading session.	RL For the first time ever, Robert asked to join the writer's circle today.	JB Brought in a letter written at home for the class post box — for class friend.

Figure 6.30: Sample adhesive-note recordings

• Cross-curriculum Grids

Prepared observation grids allow teachers to quickly record any
observations of the selected group of students across a range of
curriculum areas. Multiple copies of the observation grid may be
needed if the teacher is observing students over an entire week.

Cross-curriculum Grid					
Teacher _____ Class _____ Date _____					
Names	**Technology**	**Mathematics**	**Society and Environment**	**Science**	**Music**
Susan					
Marco					
Janette					
Phillip					
Jack					
Stephan					

Figure 6.31: Cross-curriculum grid

2 Checklists

A checklist, as the name suggests, is a list of skills or behaviours to be checked off as they are observed. Many teachers use checklists to help focus their assessment on particular literacy behaviours. Whether teacher-made or commercially produced, it is critical to acknowledge that checklists are static. Students will change over the course of a year and therefore the checklists will also need to change. Most checklists will not be applicable to every student in the classroom, particularly when there is a wide range of abilities.

Checklist for Report Writing	Always	Sometimes	Not Yet	Teacher's Comments
Purpose The writer: • demonstrates understanding that there are different types of reports and that the structure of a report depends on the purpose for which it is written • demonstrates understanding that reports contain information that is selected, sorted and synthesised to give the reader/writer information significant to a topic or focus of study				
Text Organisation and Content The writer: • uses report framework and adapts it to suit purpose and audience *Classification* • writes an introduction that successfully classifies and/or generalises information essential to the subject of the report • uses accurate definitions *Descriptions* • includes detailed information selected because of its relevance to the subject of the report • elaborates on and interprets important information • organises like information into paragraphs that link cohesively in logical order *Conclusion* • writes a conclusion that accurately identifies the main points				
Language Features The writer: • uses a formal and objective style • demonstrates consistent use of tense (usually timeless present tense); e.g. are, hunt, fly, live, suckle • demonstrates consistent use of singular or plural generic participants; e.g. humanity faces increasing... the family is ... • uses generic terms successfully; e.g. humankind, mammals, pollutants • uses a range of precise subject-specific terms in context • uses precise descriptive language • uses linking verbs, e.g. has a, is a, belongs to • uses appropriate language to compare, contrast, define or classify, e.g. identical, related, kindred				

Barrier Game: Checklist of Behaviours

Name: Date:

Class:

Rating   1: not evident   2: developing   3: fully adequate

Giving Instructions			
Organises self for task; e.g. sorting materials	1	2	3
Gives appropriate instructions that are intelligible, complete, specific	1	2	3
Uses appropriate vocabulary: • naming	1	2	3
• attribute words	1	2	3
• location words	1	2	3
Modifies instructions spontaneously, or at the listener's request	1	2	3
Checks location of items at end of game and gives feedback to listener	1	2	3

Receiving Instructions			
Follows instructions	1	2	3
Scans and locates items efficiently	1	2	3
Asks for clarification of unclear instructions	1	2	3
Indicates when instructions have been carried out	1	2	3

Figure 6.32: Sample checklists

115

3 Rubrics

Rubrics are recording frameworks that feature short descriptive statements along a continuum of excellence. Teachers and/or students can determine the quality of a performance against a set of predetermined criteria.

Levels within a rubric can be labelled using descriptive words; e.g. well developed, partially developed, not developed, or using a numerical system.

Rubrics can be refined by adding levels of achievement as students' skill level increases, or by adding additional criteria for new concepts, skills or attitudes that students display.

There are many publications and websites that offer teachers ready-made rubrics to use with their students. However, for any number of reasons, teachers may wish to create their own rubrics. Teachers can involve students in the creation of the rubrics since ultimately it is their work that is being judged. Generating criteria will enhance students' understanding of the standard of work expected.

Our News-telling Rubric: Created by Year 4				
Criteria	**SCORE 4 POINTS**	**SCORE 3 POINTS**	**SCORE 2 POINTS**	**SCORE 1 POINT**
Choosing a Topic	Chooses a range of topics that are of interest to the class	Talks about own experiences	Uses the same topics each time, e.g. my dog, my family	Gives little thought to topic
Presenting Talk	Keeps the class interested with humour, gestures, volume and pace	Speaks at an appropriate pace and volume	Speaks in short, simple sentences, but can't always be heard by the class	Often can't be heard by the class
Eye Contact	Keeps appropriate eye contact with the class at all times	Uses eye contact with the class	Sometimes looks at the class when speaking	Doesn't look at the class much
Answering Questions	Answers questions clearly and expands on information	Answers questions with enough information	Answers questions but information may be brief	Usually responds to questions with a *yes* or a *no*

Figure 6.33: Sample rubric

4 Annotations

Annotations are short judgements recorded about a student's work. These are written by the teacher directly onto the work sample. Annotations may be completed at the time of the event but can also be completed at a later time.

Annotations need to be objective, factual comments and should help a teacher to recognise and interpret individual patterns of learning over time.

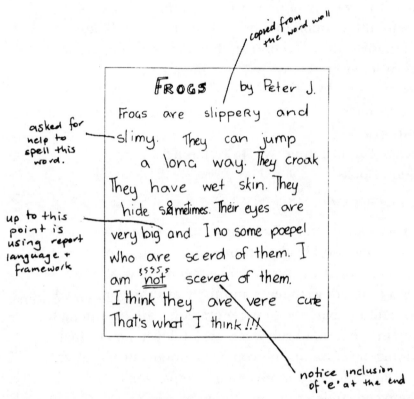

Figure 6.34: Annotated work sample

5 First Steps *Maps of Development*

The *First Steps* Maps of Development are an excellent framework for recording information about students' literacy development. Some teachers choose to record their observations, outcomes of conversations or their analysis of products directly onto the Maps of Development. This is done by highlighting Indicators displayed. Other teachers prefer to use other recording methods first; e.g. **anecdotal notes, annotations or rubrics**. This recorded information is then transferred onto the Maps of Development. Either way is effective.

How Can the Information Be Shared with Others?

As teachers become more and more skilled at gathering valuable information about students' development, it becomes equally important, when appropriate, to be able to share that information effectively with others. Traditionally report cards were the most common method of sharing information with parents, other teachers and the student. However, many teachers are experimenting with a variety of new ways to communicate valid, reliable and useful information to others. Schools, as a whole, are looking for alternative ways to report student achievement without using numbers or letter grade scores. These include:

• Report Cards
• Portfolios and E-folios
• Learning Journeys
• Student/Teacher/Parent (Three-way) Conferences
• Communication Books.

1 Report Cards

Report card formats are continually being developed and designed by districts and schools worldwide. Report card reform is often a result of teachers identifying a mismatch between the ways they are assessing and evaluating students and the ways they are asked to report information to parents. New report forms are beginning to portray learning in the form of rubrics, maps of development that include behaviours or indicators, outcome statements or narratives. Newly designed report formats rarely make comparisons of achievement between students but put an emphasis on documenting individual accomplishments.

2 Portfolios and E-folios

Portfolios provide an excellent alternative or addition to regular reporting formats often used in schools. Portfolios are a collection of student work samples that have been completed over time as part of ongoing daily classroom tasks. Collections usually include some form of evaluative comments by the teacher and student.

Collated work samples provide tangible evidence of individual development over time and discourage competitive comparisons being made between students. A picture of what a child has learnt can be clearly seen by teachers, parents and others through a portfolio collection.

Teachers usually support students in the selection of pieces to be included in a portfolio. The goal should always be to illustrate growth in the best possible way. It is recommended to include a balance of process and product work samples.

3 Learning Journeys

Learning journeys are a way for students to report learning to others. They provide an opportunity not only to report on what has been learnt but also on the way it was learnt. Properly executed, a learning journey is more than a 'show and tell' of work samples. They can provide an opportunity for students to report on:

- activities in the classroom; e.g. shared writing
- games; e.g. barrier games
- learning centres or areas; e.g. science table
- environmental print; e.g. cumulative charts
- independent work areas; e.g. writing table, reading corner.

Note: See Chapter 9: 'The Metacognitive Process' for further information on Learning Journeys.

4 Three-way Conferences

Three-way conferences allow the teacher, parent and student all to have input into a discussion about the student's development over time. They provide an ideal opportunity for reporting and sharing information with parents. These conferences can be led by the student and may incorporate a 'journey' around the classroom, pre-conference observation of the student in the classroom setting and/or the sharing of a portfolio collection.

Note: See Chapter 10: 'Communicating with Parents' for further information on Three-way Conferences.

5 Communication Books

Communication books have been used successfully as a form of two-way sharing between the home and the classroom. Each student has a personal communication book that allows the teacher and parents to share comments. These may be in praise of a particular achievement, may focus on one area, or may offer general comments about the student. Parents can be encouraged to exchange comments with the teacher, providing information about literacy development in the home setting.

Communication Book

Jack Mahler

-Page 5-

17th March

Dear Louise and Bruce,
Wanted to let you know that Jack made a huge step with his writing today. Jack, for the first time, wrote his own entire story. He has done a fantastic job of using invented spelling in this retell. Please praise him as much as you can about this.
Thanks
Jane.

Thanks for sharing this news, Jane. It truly was a marvellous effort. Is it OK if we keep the work at home for the week as Jack's grandma is coming to visit and we would love to share it with her?
Louise

2nd May.

Louise,
Please feel free to return Jack's work next week. Thanks for volunteering to join us on our trip to the zoo. Is it possible for you to join the class on Monday afternoon prior to the excursion? I am hoping to work with the children to create a plan for the day including a map of our movement around the zoo.
It would be great if you could join us then.
Jane.

Figure 6.35: Sample page from communication book

CHAPTER 7

Effective Teaching and Learning Practices

Why Label Teaching Practices?

Effective teaching and learning is made up of numerous behaviours, most so intricately woven in a personal, professional and contextualised way that making them explicit is a difficult task. As all behaviours are socially and culturally determined, some appear so natural as to need no analysis. However, examining teaching and learning practices can:

- be a springboard for critical reflection, leading to the refinement of a flexible and strategic teaching or learning repertoire
- help teachers and students recognise and support different learning preferences and styles
- expose some practices as more culturally appropriate than others
- help teachers to maintain a focus on teaching and learning rather than testing, and 'busy work'.

The teaching and learning practices explained in this chapter exclude 'telling' and 'testing'.

Telling is defined as the verbal delivery of information by the teacher.

Testing is defined as the examination of performance under controlled conditions.

Although commonplace in many schools, 'telling' and 'testing' may be ineffective for teaching and learning unless combined with other practices. Furthermore, the advantages and disadvantages of both are generally well known to teachers. Deciding when to teach, tell or problem-solve is part of the intricate art of teaching.

Learning and teaching practices are without boundaries. Teachers and students bend, shape, adapt and blend them to achieve a variety of purposes. Ideally this manipulation and crafting is done strategically, but in reality time, resources, the curriculum, the context and sociocultural values influence teaching and learning practices in profound ways. The spontaneity of the classroom means teaching and learning practices frequently merge to the extent that they are sometimes difficult to recognise. This is a positive process when managed effectively. Isolating individual practices simply serves the purpose of assisting teachers and learners to reflect on the effectiveness of each.

What Is a Practice?

A practice is a socially and culturally determined way of interacting with others in the name of teaching and/or learning. Many practices are described in collective terms. For example, the term 'Sharing' is used to describe a wide range of teaching procedures that have something in common, such as Shared Reading and Shared Writing. Sharing is considered a practice because it represents the scaffolding that occurs when a teacher and student engage in the joint construction of meaning. It is applicable to all areas of teaching and learning. Shared Writing, however, is labelled a procedure. It consists of a number of widely accepted steps or stages in the joint construction of a text. Of course, whether a practice is primarily a teaching or learning practice is in the eye of the beholder. When students use a teaching practice such as 'modelling' to share skills with a peer, they rarely do so without deepening their own learning.

Details on specific teaching procedures are to be found in the individual strand Resource Books. For example, Shared Reading is explained in the Reading Resource Book, Guided Viewing in the Viewing Resource Book.

Understanding Effective Teaching and Learning Practices

Effective teaching and learning practices provide a useful guide for decision-making when linking assessment to teaching. Having placed students on a Map of Development, teachers use the Major Teaching Emphases to direct the choice of learning experiences. The process of selecting procedures or phase-specific activities becomes more strategic when teachers understand the relative strengths and weaknesses of a wide range of teaching practices. Consider the following Major Teaching Emphasis.

Teach the use of conventions of print, e.g. commas, quotation marks.

Given that the Major Teaching Emphasis has not provided a key word like 'model', 'analyse' or 'practise', there is scope for an enormous range of procedures and/or phase-specific activities to be employed. A repertoire of effective teaching and learning practices enables a teacher to be strategic about the selection of an activity. If students have had little previous exposure to particular conventions of print a sequence of modelling, sharing and guiding may be appropriate. However, if some prior knowledge is evident, problem-solving, using analysing as a teaching practice, might be more suitable. When teachers and students become familiar with effective teaching and learning practices they are empowered to employ these strategically in a range of contexts, strands and learning areas.

Some of the practices are often used in a complementary way, with particular sequences being used to good effect. For instance, modelling, sharing and guiding have been used prominently in reading as a means of moving students from a very supportive context in which the teacher has a high degree of control (modelling) to a more independent context in which the teacher plays a role that is more about facilitation (guiding).

The Gradual Release of Responsibility Through the Use of Teaching and Learning Practices

	Modelling	Sharing	Guiding	Applying
Role of the Teacher	The teacher demonstrates by thinking aloud the processes used.	The teacher provides the direction and invites the students to contribute.	The teacher scaffolds help and provides support and corrective feedback.	The teacher offers support and encouragement as necessary.
Degree of Control			Students do the work with help from the teacher or other sources at predetermined points.	Students work independently. They are in control of the ideas and the information.
Role of the Students	Students participate by actively attending to the demonstrations.	Students contribute ideas and information. Decision-making is negotiated between teacher and student.		

Figure 7.1

Combining teaching practices in a strategic way makes perfect sense, and enables teachers to maximise a repertoire of teaching practices. However, to employ modelling, for example, only at the beginning of a unit of work is to ignore students' need for frequent demonstrations at other key points in the teaching and learning process. While experimenting with the compatibility of effective teaching and learning practices, it is essential that teachers be alert to the versatility of each. What makes a teaching and learning practice effective is its appropriateness for the needs of students in a particular context.

Description of Effective Teaching and Learning Practices

The following Effective Teaching and Learning Practices deliberately involve active engagement by students. 'Doing' something with a text is a powerful way for the brain to get to grips with the learning.

First Steps Definitions of Effective Teaching and Learning Practices	
Familiarising	raising awareness and activating prior knowledge
Modelling	thinking aloud to show how and why something is done
Sharing	jointly constructing meaning
Guiding	providing scaffolding through strategic assistance at predetermined checkpoints
Analysing	examining the parts in order to understand the whole
Practising	rehearsing a skill or strategy
Applying	independently using a skill, strategy or understanding to achieve a purpose
Investigating	finding, analysing, questioning and using information for a purpose
Playing	exploring concepts and skills through imagining and creating
Discussing	exchanging opinions about topics, themes and issues
Innovating	altering or amending an existing text
Transforming	re-creating a text or object in another genre, form, mode, medium or format
Simulating	adopting a role in a hypothetical situation
Reflecting	thinking about the what, how and why of experiences

Figure 7.2

Familiarising

Purpose: To raise awareness and activate prior knowledge

Description

Familiarising, sometimes referred to as immersing or exposure, is a generic term used to describe the way in which teachers introduce students to an area of learning. Generally, familiarising involves students reading, listening to or viewing specific subject matter. The discussion to activate prior knowledge following this exposure is also included. More examples of the subject matter are sometimes collected, compared and displayed by both teacher and students over time, building up an awareness of features of the learning focus. Many other experiences of a preliminary or preparatory nature, including incursions and excursions, fit under the heading of familiarising.

Key Features

- Includes a range of receptive experiences
- Builds knowledge
- Activates prior knowledge
- Exposes students to a variety of texts that have something in common
- Builds an awareness of examples of texts in daily life
- Involves ongoing discussion of examples in daily life

Using Familiarising in the Classroom

Although familiarising could be accurately described as 'awareness raising', it is a mistake to consider it a passive teaching and learning practice. Reading, listening and viewing are active sociocultural behaviours. There is a greater need for the student to become actively engaged when an activity is undertaken to familiarise, because it is through this engagement that the student will gain an understanding of the features of the focus. For example, a teacher keen to familiarise a class with the features of interviewing may arrange to view a video of a famous person being interviewed. It is inevitable that, in enjoying the experience, many students may focus on the content of what the star has to say, rather than the nature of the questions and comments of the interviewer. Reviewing and pausing may be required to help students distance themselves from the content of the text and engage with the interviewing techniques. Students may then be requested to collect examples of interviews for use in further activities such as deconstructing the text.

A Collection of Interviews		
Borrow this video to see an interview with Adam Williams.	Magazine Interview with Adam Williams **Interviewer:** Well, Adam, how did you get started ...? Adam: It was like this ...	Visit these websites for great interviews with the stars! www.abd.com www.xyz.com.au

Figure 7.3

Modelling

Purpose: To demonstrate the thinking processes behind how and why something is done

Description

Consider any skill that we teach to another person in everyday life, such as sewing on a button or driving a car, and think about the key teaching practice that is used. It is modelling. The proficient person shows the learner what to do, often talking the learner through the steps. Although it is possibly the oldest and most popular teaching practice in the world, modelling can vary greatly in its effectiveness according to its execution. Much hinges on whether the demonstration is explicit, whether it has a clear focus and whether it includes targeted 'think-aloud' statements that provide learners with an insight into the complex cognitive processes that underpin the skill.

Before students are expected to apply any new learning, it is critical that they are actively involved in multiple demonstrations. In learning situations it is appropriate for the proficient person to conclude demonstrations with the comment, 'Now you have a go'.

Key Features

- Brevity (5–10 minutes, depending on students' attention span)
- Locus of control with the teacher
- Clear 'think-aloud' statements
- Singular or limited focus
- Repetition
- Connection between modelling sessions

Modelling a craft

Using Modelling in the Classroom

'Think-aloud' statements are central to the success of modelling. It is often the case that statements declare the *outcome* of the thinking when it is the *process* of thinking that is the critical aspect. For example, a modelled reading lesson designed to teach the skill of self-correction could include the following:

> **Text on whiteboard:** Some fish <u>canneries</u> print a 'dolphin-friendly' label ...
>
> **Teacher (reading):** Some fish <u>canaries</u> print a 'dolphin-friendly' label ...
>
> Hang on, that doesn't sound right ... fish canaries? Let me check that. I'll break that word up — fish can-neries ... oh, maybe it's like a factory where they put the fish into cans for food or pet food ... now that makes more sense.
>
> **Teacher (re-reading):** Some fish <u>canneries</u> print a 'dolphin-friendly' label ...

The explanation provides much more insight into how the self-correction is arrived at than the following statement, which does not outline the leaps in logic behind the decision-making: 'Now, by self-correcting I know that word is *canneries*, not *canaries*.'

The practice of modelling is so pervasive that often students learn significantly from implicit modelling. Teachers sometimes find it difficult to crystallise the focus of a modelling session. For example, a teacher modelling how to identify an unknown word will almost certainly also be modelling a love of reading, and may be tempted to talk about the content of the text. An awareness of this tendency is useful. However, for planning and teaching purposes it is most effective to concentrate on a particular focus.

Sharing

Purpose: To jointly construct meaning

Description

Sharing the accomplishment of a learning task is a cooperative and supportive way of engaging learners. In this effective teaching practice the teacher leads the demonstration of the understanding or skill. The teacher pauses at predetermined points and responds to learner prompts, thus including the learners in the task. The teacher might ask a question and encourage the learners to assist or respond to a learner-initiated query. All contributions receive a positive response. Sharing involves the teacher and learner as collaborative participants in a joint exercise, whereas modelling involves the teacher as an expert demonstrator with students as observers.

Key Features

- Interaction focused on the joint achievement of a clear purpose
- A teacher-managed blend of modelling, student input and discussion
- Negotiated decisions about the text
- A short time span (generally 10–15 minutes)
- Text visible and accessible to all
- A single or limited focus
- Targeted feedback
- Connection between sharing sessions

Shared reading session

Using Sharing in the Classroom

In sharing, the learner is like a passenger on a tandem bike, observing the skilled cyclist (the teacher), listening to that person's 'think-aloud' statements and joining in at appropriate times. The task is shared, not necessarily because each participant has an equal workload, but because they negotiate direction and participation. Although conventionally used in reading and writing, sharing is a teaching and learning practice that can provide useful scaffolding for students in speaking and listening, and, with a little adaptation, also in viewing. Through negotiation and collaboration the process of comprehending or composing is shared by the teacher and students. The teacher usually leads the dialogue with probing questions to stimulate comprehension or creation of the text, providing advice only when it is required. Some shared writing practices differ on who holds the pen, but ultimately what is important is who provides the direction for the comprehension or creation of the text.

Guiding

Purpose: To provide scaffolded support through strategic assistance at predetermined checkpoints

Description

Guiding is a practice that involves the teacher explicitly scaffolding a task. This could be through removing distracting or difficult elements, dividing the task into more manageable parts or providing strategic assistance at key points. The student maintains control of the process, but is able to request assistance at any point.

Key Features

- Frequent support and opportunities for teacher–student interaction
- Frameworks that scaffold the task; e.g. note-taking templates, questioning patterns
- Decisions made by students
- Targeted feedback supplied at predetermined stages
- A singular or limited focus for each student–teacher interaction

Using Guiding in the Classroom

Guiding differs from sharing in that the student is performing the task. To continue the bike analogy, guiding involves the student riding a cycle of his or her own, while being carefully watched by a mentor who monitors the distances travelled and steadies the wobbling cyclist when necessary. In guided procedures and activities the task may be structured by the teacher to include opportunities for assistance but the completion of the task is controlled by the student.

The degree of guidance will be dependent on the student, the context and the nature of the task. For instance, in Guided Reading, the teacher may choose to have students in a small group reading short sections of the same text, stopping periodically to clarify, question and predict. However, more independence could be apparent in a Guided Writing procedure. Students may use plans or other frameworks to complete an individual task in which the teacher provides feedback at regular intervals throughout the writing process.

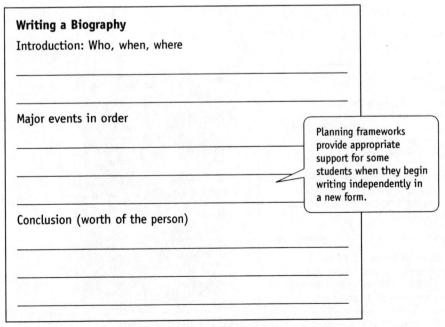

Writing a Biography
Introduction: Who, when, where

_____

_____

Major events in order

_____

Planning frameworks provide appropriate support for some students when they begin writing independently in a new form.

_____

_____

Conclusion (worth of the person)

_____

_____

_____

Figure 7.4: A framework used in Guided Writing

Analysing

Purpose: To examine the parts in order to understand the whole

Description

Analysing is a powerful and pervasive practice involving the problem-solving, evaluating and classifying activities that require students to break texts into parts to understand their relationship with the whole. Text deconstruction, reconstruction and graphic representations of texts are examples of analysing tasks.

Key Features

- A focus on the relationship between parts and whole (letters within words, sentences within paragraphs, paragraphs in written texts; colours, objects and positioning within visual texts)
- A focus on the attributes of language features, often through classification
- An open-ended search for patterns and features

Using Analysing in the Classroom

The human brain is geared to search for and identify patterns. The use of analysing practices is a very effective way of teaching and learning for deep understanding. However, not all texts or text parts have recognisable patterns. For example, although some paragraphs begin with a topic sentence that sums up the main idea, followed by supporting detail, many do not. Teachers and students, when analysing, need to be aware of the fluid and diverse nature of language, and also of the limitations of applying understanding about patterns to new contexts. The predominant features of a narrative text in a Western society, for instance, may not be apparent in a narrative generated in another culture.

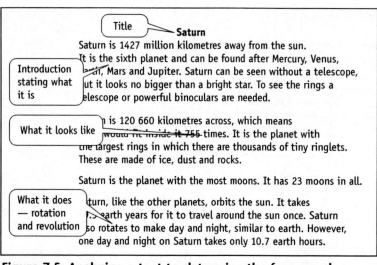

Figure 7.5: Analysing a text to determine the framework

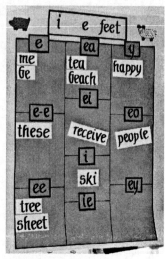

Word-sorting chart

Practising

Purpose: To rehearse a skill or strategy to promote proficiency

Description

Practising is the term given to all activities in which a particular skill is being rehearsed. Completion of a story map or a punctuation exercise is practice. Practising means that a skill or strategy has been given emphasis in an activity, sometimes by isolating it from whole texts. Effective teachers ensure that a practice activity is preceded by modelling, sharing or guiding, and supported by structures that scaffold the task. For example, students completing a cloze task already know that a number of words can make sense in the space and, more importantly, are familiar with a range of strategies to work out what word would make sense in the context. Exercises in which a skill is being practised without support, or where the emphasis is placed on the outcome, as opposed to process, are effectively tests of prior knowledge.

Key Features

- A focus on the process of rehearsing a skill or strategy with the idea of promoting proficiency
- Support in the form of prior teaching or targeted feedback
- Prior discussion about the use of strategies

Using Practising in the Classroom

The effectiveness of purposeful practice can usually be gauged by the degree of similarity between the procedure or activity, and the independent application of the skill. For example, a teacher wishing to help a student acquire a bank of sight words will need to decide whether the use of flashcards mimics the contextualised act of reading more effectively than any other practice method. Although reading and writing are complex acts made up of numerous behaviours that could benefit from practice, some of these behaviours can become distorted or irrelevant in isolation.

DAY ONE: PRACTICE ACTIVITIES

1 Print your list words into your pad.
   Put a circle around the tricky part in each word.

   Example: w h (a) t

   ❋ ❋ ❋ ❋

2 Print each word again.
   How do the letter shapes look?
   Use your coloured pencil to show them.

   Example: w h a t

   ❋ ❋ ❋ ❋

3 See if you can make some new words by changing a letter.

   Example: w h a t ⟶ t h a t

Figure 7.6: Sample practice activities, focus on spelling

It is important that students understand how and why the activity fits into the bigger scheme of things. The teacher may, for instance, discuss with them how Assisted Reading (see Reading Resource Book) can help develop fluency and expression, or how completing a cloze activity provides an opportunity to practise writing sight words.

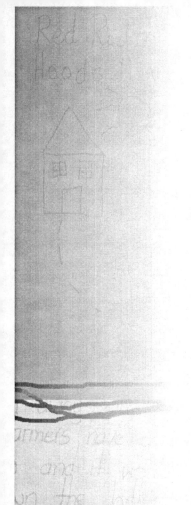

Applying

Purpose: To use independently a skill, strategy or understanding to achieve a purpose

Description

Applying refers to the contextualised and purposeful use of reading, writing, speaking and listening, or viewing. Such acts are whole and focused, with a purpose and audience, and generally involve the student making ongoing decisions independently. Applying practices are normally seen as an end point in a teaching cycle because they represent full student independence. Access to teacher advice is not denied, yet neither is it planned or structured in a way that indicates reliance. Applying practices are commonly used by teachers as pseudo-assessment tasks. When structured appropriately they can reflect how a student performs without assistance. However, a range of applying tasks is necessary for a teacher to form sound judgements and conclusions.

Key Features

- Minimal teacher support for the student
- Application of learning to a different context
- Need for the student to address factors of context such as authentic purpose and audience

Using Applying in the Classroom

Applying practices are deceptively difficult to organise. Students assigned independent writing tasks to be completed for a teacher appear to be applying their skills, understandings and attitudes. Yet contextual factors such as the selection and refinement of topic, or the choice of purpose and audience are sometimes omitted. For students to be truly applying their skills, teachers need to find opportunities in school that replicate the multiple demands of literacy events in real life.

Students are applying their knowledge when they:
- choose from a range of known forms in response to a task
- use what is learnt from the jointly negotiated writing of a text when writing in that form independently
- apply what is learnt in one context to a different context; e.g. **using strategies demonstrated in Guided Reading when reading a science book**
- make use of what is learnt from working with one text when working with another.

Investigating

Purpose: To find, analyse, question and use information for a purpose

Description

Investigating occurs when the teacher prompts students to gather information beyond their current knowledge. Researching, hypothesising and inquiring are synonymous with investigating. This may involve interviewing members of the community, drawing information from the Internet or comparing articles from newspapers. Traditionally investigating practices have consisted mainly of projects in other curriculum areas, involving the collection of facts and information. However, investigating practices have more recently been used to assist students in more versatile ways. For example, students using texts retrieved from the Internet have questioned authors' motives and the persuasive techniques they have used, rather than simply gathering information.

Key Features

- A clear question or hypothesis to be tested
- Use of a range of spoken, written and visual texts

Using Investigating in the Classroom

Investigating practices generally fall into two categories. The first involves searching for examples of texts or text components to find patterns and make generalisations. For example, a teacher might ask students to collect business letters to investigate the format used. This investigating gradually unfolds into analysing as students compare parts of the letter layouts. The second category includes the research of a particular topic for a purpose. Students might search for information about the leading lifestyle diseases in the nation to answer a focus question generated during health studies. This type of investigating relies heavily on note-taking and the synthesising of information, requiring substantial teaching of these skills.

Investigating Spiders			
Know	Want	How	Learn
What do I know?	What do I want to find out?	How can I find out what I want to learn?	What did I learn?
• Spiders have 8 legs. • Spiders make webs. • Redback spiders are poisonous.	• How do spiders make webs? • What is the web made of? • How many poisonous spiders are there?	• Check in library for CD-Rom, books about spiders. • Ask the class spider expert. • Go to the website National Geographic for Kids.	

> Complete at conclusion of investigation

Figure 7.7: Using a KWHL chart as a framework for investigating

Playing

Purpose: To explore concepts and skills by imagining and creating

Description

Play, both structured and unstructured, involves the learner exploring concepts and skills by imagining and creating, trying out ideas and reflecting on successes and difficulties. It can involve experimentation with text forms in a play corner, or contributions to a class speaking-and-listening game. Students frequently draw on their experiences of play and use them in their literacy behaviour.

Unstructured play is the spontaneous, free engagement of the student, often with others, but with no ongoing involvement of the teacher. The environment may invite particular sorts of play and the teacher may model the sorts of literacy behaviours associated with that environment but students control and direct their own activity. An example of this is a small part of a classroom simulating a place such as a doctor's surgery and its specific literacy. Students may use the appropriate clothes and props to role-play interactions between doctors and patients, writing prescriptions and posing questions.

Structured play is guided by the teacher, the context or the resources. It may involve frequent prompts, specific resources with guidelines or a game with established rules.

Key Features of Unstructured Play

- A language-rich and literacy-rich environment that stimulates experimentation
- Time and opportunity to explore

Key Features of Structured Play

- Identifiable rules and roles
- Focus on the use of an understanding or skill
- Outcomes based on varying degrees of skill, knowledge and chance

Using Playing in the Classroom

Unstructured play should be seen as worthwhile. As students interact with each other, they are engaged in social practice. When they engage with literacy resources, they are engaged with the social practice of literacy. For example, in the class 'restaurant' the 'customers' can be seen studying the menu, the 'waiters' are writing the orders and the 'chef' is listening to the orders and giving instructions on how to cook the food. When students are involved in such spontaneous play they respond to the situation with increased engagement and persistence because they are motivated to do so. The level of engagement and persistence may have been less if this had been a teacher-directed activity.

Despite implying fun, some sorts of play can become onerous for students. Structured playing of games that require players to use prior knowledge alone are effectively tests in disguise. Similarly, word-play opportunities that are unsupported by strategies to help students generate and manipulate words and word parts place an enormous cognitive burden on some students. Structured games that emphasise the use of support teamwork, that are preceded by effective teaching, and that employ an element of chance are the most constructive.

Discussing

Purpose: To exchange opinions about topics, themes and issues

Description

Discussing involves the exchange of opinions about topics, themes and issues, and the reshaping that occurs when these are shared in groups or as a whole class. It differs from students' responses to questions that are closed or require specific answers. Students' responses to texts may differ according to their prior experience and knowledge.

Key Features

- Open-ended questions to stimulate discussion
- Use of group discussion processes such as turn-taking, role-adoption and response routines
- A shared focus — what is being discussed for what reason

Using Discussing in the Classroom

Effective discussion results from a caring and collaborative classroom culture, supportive group dynamics, agreed group processes and a shared focus. The qualities of a caring and collaborative classroom, as described in Chapter 5: 'Establishing a Positive Teaching and Learning Environment', ensure that students feel confident about contributing opinions and receiving feedback. However, it is not unusual for a small group of speakers to dominate discussions or for some students to be reluctant to share their thoughts. It is the teacher's role to nurture group dynamics that are balanced and supportive. This can be done by teaching the processes for discussion (see Speaking and Listening Resource Book).

Book Discussion Group

These processes include turn-taking, adoption of roles, and routines for responding. Finally, a shared focus is important to productive discussions. Open discussions serve a valid purpose in enabling students to share feelings and brainstorm ideas, but discussions without clear aims are rarely helpful in the context of a planned curriculum. **Book Discussion Groups** (see Reading Resource Book) and **Authors' Circles** (see Writing Resource Book) provide opportunities for students to engage in meaningful discussions.

Innovating

Purpose: To alter or amend certain features of an existing text

Description

Innovating involves altering or amending an existing text to create a new one. Innovating implies that the structure of the original text is maintained but new content is used. 'Text Innovation' is the obvious example, yet many other activities that do not carry this label exist. For example, when a group of students parody a TV quiz show for an assembly item, or put new words to an existing popular tune they are innovating.

Key Features

- Enjoyment and analysis of the conventions of a text
- Discussion about patterns, features or conventions to be adapted
- Presentation, publication or performance of the innovated text

Using Innovating in the Classroom

Innovating is a powerful teaching and learning practice because it gives students permission to copy existing texts in an appropriate way. The challenge for students is to find the patterned aspects of a text that make it appealing and perhaps unique. In doing so they use analysis to become aware of the structure of the text and the features that make it work. Innovating is a way of scaffolding that allows students to use the work of authors as a foundation to experiment with the parts of a text they can manage.

Text Innovations on Nursery Rhymes

Hush little baby, don't make a noise Papa's going to buy you a box of toys. If that box of toys gets old, Papa's going to buy you a bar of gold…	Twinkle, twinkle little star, What is in the cookie jar? Chocolate chip or sugar spice, Peanut crunchies — oh, they're nice! Twinkle, twinkle little star, What is in the cookie jar?

Text Innovations on 'Alligator Pie'

Alligator cake, Alligator cake If I don't get some, my heart is gonna break Give away my French fries, give away my shake But don't give away my alligator cake.	Stegosaurus steak, Stegosaurus steak If I don't get some, I'll have a tummy ache Give away my cream bun, give away my cake But don't give away my Stegosaurus steak.

Transforming

Purpose: To re-create a text or object in another genre, form, mode, medium or format

Description

Transforming refers to the re-creation of a text in another genre, form, mode, medium or format. This will only be successful if the student has some level of control over the structure and features of the new text.

Key Features

- An authentic purpose for transforming a text
- Prior teaching of the conventions of the two different forms, modes or media
- Reflection about new perspectives created by the new form, mode or medium

Using Transforming in the Classroom

The process of transforming a text is a most effective way of demonstrating thorough comprehension. However, most transformations are more difficult than they look. At the very least the student needs to be able to comprehend the original text, particularly grasping its structure, features and content. The consequent challenge is to re-create the meaning of the original text in a different way. For example, a student asked to dramatise a scene from a literary text will rely heavily on understandings about dramatic techniques.

Teachers often use activities such as Readers' Theatre, Read and Retell or dramatisation as opportunities for students to transform texts. Transforming helps students develop a deeper understanding of the text as they re-create it in different ways. For example, written texts can be re-created as visual or oral interpretations.

Figure 7.8: The fairytale 'The Three Little Pigs' has been transformed into a newspaper story.

	Original Text 'The Three Little Pigs'	Transformed Text 'Pigs Outsmart Wolf'
Genre	literary	informational
Purpose	to entertain	to retell
Form	narrative	recount
Mode	written	written
Format	picture book	newspaper report
Medium	printed	printed

Simulating

Purpose: To adopt a role in a hypothetical situation

Description

Whenever students are asked to adopt a role or imagine themselves in a particular setting or set of circumstances, they are involved in simulating. This practice helps students learn about alternative viewpoints and reflect upon attitudes. Simulating sometimes involves performance, as in a debate where a student must assume a standpoint; a role-play where students act out a situation; or Readers' Theatre, where a student must read a part in character.

Key Features

- Adoption of a role or perspective
- Creation of texts from a specific viewpoint
- Justification and substantiation of opinions and perspectives

Using Simulating in the Classroom

Simulation is often used in Studies of Society and Environment because it is particularly effective in helping students reflect upon their attitudes. However, an essential part of all texts, both literary and informational, is the perspective and roles of key characters. By adopting and reflecting upon the roles of key characters students are in strong positions to understand complex texts. Teachers can assist students to look at situations from different perspectives by asking questions such as: 'What would you have done in this situation?'; 'If David had given the money back to George, how would the story have changed?'; 'How would you have handled the pollution spillage if you had been the fire chief?' Having students form groups with allocated roles allows them to explore many topics from different perspectives.

An issue about children causing problems during school holidays has been raised in the local newspaper. Some people are suggesting school holidays should be shortened to one week to reduce the problem. This issue has raised lively debate in the classroom and has provided an opportunity for the teacher to use simulation in a meaningful context.
- The teacher has put the students into groups to discuss the problem.
- Each group was allocated a role (store owners, teachers, police officers, swimming pool manager, children, movie theatre owner) and is to look at the issue from that perspective.
- Each group brainstorms the problem and solutions as seen from the allocated point of view.
- The class meets as a whole group at the conclusion to discuss the different perspectives.

Figure 7.9: Description of a simulation activity

Reflecting

Purpose: To think about the what, how and why of experiences

Description

Reflecting involves analysing and making judgements about what has been learnt and how that learning took place. For this to be successful, students need the opportunity and structures to allow them to stand back and think about what they have learnt. While some students are strategic in their use of processes and the monitoring of their learning, other students need to be explicitly taught these skills. Reflection enables students to become aware of, monitor and evaluate their learning processes and strategies.

Key Features

- Thinking about what was learnt and how it was learnt
- Making judgements about the effectiveness of the strategies employed
- Making future decisions based on those judgements

Using Reflecting in the Classroom

Reflection often happens at the end of a lesson but it can also occur during the lesson. By reiterating what has been learnt teachers can reinforce important learning. For reflection to be successful there must be something to reflect on. Explicitly stating the purpose of the lesson before beginning can provide the stimulus for the reflection at the end. Reflection can empower students as they focus on what they can do and what they know (See Chapter 9).

Student Self-Assessment
Transitional Reading Phase

Name: _____ Date: _____

First Steps: Look What I Can Do

My Reading Behaviours—I can:	Not Yet	Sometimes	Consistently
• State the main idea of a text and provide details from the text to support it			
• Discuss information that is stated in a text			
• Select information from a text for a specific purpose			
• Link ideas both stated and implied; e.g. tell about cause and effect			
• Use the library system and search engines to locate and select suitable texts for a specific purpose			
• Check the currency and relevance of information for a specific purpose			
• Tell when authors are trying to make me think about something their way			
• Tell why my interpretation of a text may be different from someone else's			
• Recognise devices that authors and illustrators use to construct meaning;			

> Students can use this sheet to reflect on and make judgements about their reading processes and strategies.

Figure 7.10: Part of a reflection sheet for transitional readers

CHAPTER 8

Classroom Planning and Grouping

Using *First Steps* for Long-term and Short-term Planning

What Is Planning?

Planning is the preparation for teaching. It involves making decisions about outcomes, content, procedures, practices and learning experiences, and about the selection of resources and assessment tools that will be used. This chapter focuses on how to use the *First Steps* materials to plan for the achievement of long-term and short-term outcomes for a range of students.

Planning is:
- a continuous process which occurs before, during and after any learning situation
- driven by ongoing assessment of student behaviours
- preparation to meet the needs of whole class, small groups and individuals
- flexible and subject to change because it reflects what is happening in the classroom
- reviewed regularly and updated as appropriate
- represented by a working document that is written primarily for the benefit of the teacher.

Why Plan?

Purposeful planning makes a difference to teaching. It enables teachers to:
- ensure there is coverage of the outcomes, standards and/or curriculum set by the education system
- cater for the needs of all students in the classroom
- maximise teaching time and efficiency by having resources readily available
- create links across the curriculum so that learning can be reinforced across all subject areas
- maximise the use of support and relief teachers and programs
- share resources, ideas and workload with other year-level teachers if collaborative planning occurs
- feel confident because they are organised and prepared.

Considerations for Planning

- Be aware of student needs and individual differences — placement on the *First Steps* Map of Development will assist in identifying these.
- Be thoroughly familiar with the content to be covered and outcomes to be achieved.
- Have a repertoire of effective teaching and learning practices (see Chapter 7).
- Know about the physical aspects of the school — what equipment and resources are available.
- Consider appropriate assessment tools (see Chapter 6).

Levels of Planning

Planning looks very different for each teacher in every classroom. There is no single 'right way' to plan. Planning is often talked about as though it is one document; however, in reality planning is a process that is represented by several documents, each serving a different purpose, covering various time spans and with differing amounts of detail. All documents relate to each other and generally each level deals with a shorter time span and provides more detail of classroom activity than the previous one. The amount of documentation used in Long-term Planning, Short-term Planning and Daily Planning will vary from teacher to teacher.

Figure 8.1

Pro-formas (prepared formats) are a useful way of recording information in a compact, concise and easy-to-read way. Effective teachers make use of pro-formas at all levels of the planning process. Pro-formas need to make sense to the person using them and be user-friendly for others such as support and relief teachers. All examples shown in this chapter and those for each strand CD-ROM focus on using *First Steps* to support literacy planning at all levels. They have worked well for the teachers who have created them but should be adapted to suit individual needs and preferences.

Long-term Planning

Long-term planning gives cohesion and sets the direction for the year's activities and as such provides an overview. Teachers begin the year with some general knowledge about the strengths and needs of their students and the knowledge, skills and attitudes they must or would like to teach. The yearly overview allows for this information to be recorded. Teachers of the same year level benefit from planning collaboratively and sharing ideas, tasks and resources. By its very nature, long-term planning needs to be carried out early in the school year.

Long-term planning could include a range of elements.
- The teacher's beliefs about literacy learning and teaching.
- A class profile of student needs and strengths — *First Steps* Maps of Development from the previous year would be an excellent starting point.
- Outcomes to be worked towards — these often come directly from the outcomes, standards or curriculum frameworks that the education system has outlined.
- A list of cultural activities or special celebrations that either the school or class will be involved in during the year; e.g. a history focus selected for a unit of work leading up to a national day.
- An overview of integrated units of work — teachers can base these on a particular topic, theme, season or genre. This overview plan allows for integrating literacy across other subject areas, and it allows time to collect relevant resources, plan excursions and involve parents and other community members.
- Details of classroom organisation — including layout and timetable.
- Ways of assessing and collecting data.

A Teacher's Long-term Plan

Integrated Planning Program Overview | **Theme/Unit:** Novel- Rowan of Rin | **Level:** Junior (Middle) Upper

OVERARCHING OUTCOMES ① 2 ③ ④ 5 6 7 8 9 10 11 12 ⑬ | **VALUES** 1 2 3 4 5

LEARNING AREA OUTCOMES

ENGLISH	MATHEMATICS	THE ARTS	SOCIETY & ENVIRONMENT	SCIENCE	TECHNOLOGY & ENTERPRISE	HEALTH & PHYSICAL EDUCATION	LOTE
Writing- 2·1, 3·1, 2·2 3·2, 2·3, 3·3, 2·4, 3·4 Reading- 2·1, 3·1, 2·2, 3·2, 2·3, 3·3, 2·4, 3·4 Viewing- 2·2, 3·2 Speaking/Listening 2·2, 3·3, 2·4, 3·4		Communicating Art Ideas Level 3. Skills, Techniques & Processes Level 3.	Place & Space 2·1, 3·1, 3·2 Resources 3·1	Energy & change 1·3 Earth & Beyond 3.	Technology Process 2·1, 3·2, 3·3, 3·4 Materials 2·1, 3·1.		

LEARNING EXPERIENCES

Shared Writing
- Rowan's Journal
- Recount events add entries as story unfolds

Mapping
- Chn create their own map of Rin
- Investigate types of maps, keys, legends.
- Practise reading maps.

Mood, Music & Instruments
- Use the technology process to investigate sounds, types of music.
- Devise & produce music
- Evaluate instrument and create mood music for a scene from the novel.
- Investigate water music (sounds from jars, water levels)
- Research instruments
- Design, make and evaluate instrument (class performance)

Writing- Magic Verse
- Chn work in groups to write a verse
- Explore rhyme/rhythm through riddles in novel

Novel- Rowan of Rin

Places to Live
- Discuss why people of Rin live where they do.
- Look at WA maps & where people live
- Map WA's population, include waterways, mining, farming, cities
- Compare a European country & map the same
- Compare and contrast with semantic grid

Narrative Writing
- Chn plan and write a narrative
- Make comparisons between narratives read in shared reading & co-operative reading.
- Discuss common features & make a grid to compare.
- Sequencing - re-arrange jumbled sentences & paragraphs to make a story.
- Sentence expansion use adjectives/ adverbs to expand sentences
- Plan and write narrative- focus on one section each session.

PRINCIPLES OF LEARNING AND TEACHING
- Opportunity to learn
- Connection and challenge
- Action and reflection
- Inclusivity and difference
- Motivation and purpose
- Independence and collaboration
- Supportive environment

LITERACY FOCUS
Writing - Narrative
Rhyming words (P+T)
Paragraphs (main idea)(c)
Varied sentence beginnings (Ex+Ea)
Homonyns/homophones (P)
Sort words related by meaning (T)
Expanding sentences (Ea + c)
Editing
Goal Setting
Reading - Cooperative Reading
(Narrative focus)
Discussion Manager
Character development
Settings

Code Breaker
- Text innovation synonyms, antonyms, more interesting words
Investigator
- Cause & effect, change on event
- What is the effect
- gender stereotypes
Illustrator
- Prediction, character collage (draw things that relate to / important to character, family tree
Viewing - view visual text to see relationship between mood & music

Speaking/Listening-
- Listen for sounds, music types

Key: Spelling - P: Phonetic, T: Transitional | **Writing: Ex: experimental, Ea: early, c: conventional.**

PRINCIPLES OF ASSESSMENT
- Valid • Educative • Explicit • Fair • Comprehensive

Assessment

Student Assessment:
- Self- assessment of musical instrument
- Reflection on technology process
- Self- assessment of group - work for Magic verse.

Teacher Assessment:
- Narrative - First Steps Continua
- Technology Process - Musical instrument
- Mapping skills, semantic grid
- Cooperative Reading - First Steps continua

RESOURCES
Rowan of Rin by Emily Rhodda

EXAMPLES
Rubric
Checklist
Self-assessment
Peer assessment
Project
Observations
Test
Artefact/work samples
Journals
Photos/video/recordings

LEARNING TECHNOLOGIES
- **PRESENTATION**
  Kid Pix, Power Point, Hyperstudio, Authorware
- **PUBLISHING**
  Word, Creative Writer, Printmaster, digital camera
- **INFORMATION**
  WWW, CD rom, library, videos
- **COMMUNICATION**
  Telephone, fax, e-mail, snail mail, video conference, digital camera

Figure 8.2: Overview of an integrated unit of work (courtesy of Shannon Pearce, Australia)

Short-term Planning

Short-term planning involves the elaboration and more specific focusing of information from the long-term plan. Short-term planning* usually covers a four-to-six-week period, although the length of time is entirely a teacher's choice. Figure 8.3 illustrates the elements that may be included. Teachers consider:

- the selection of outcomes and Major Teaching Emphases
- the content, theme or topic (entry point)
- a selection of sequenced teaching and learning experiences for a whole class, small groups and, if necessary, individuals
- the resources to be used
- the assessment tools to be used.

Teachers decide whether the short-term plan might focus on a particular theme or topic, text form, school or community event or an identified common need as an entry point. Short-term planning enables teachers to consider how literacy can be taught across the curriculum. Students can see the relevance of what they are learning if the connections between learning areas are made explicit. For example, if the health curriculum deals with the issue of smoking, the literacy planning for that period could focus on writing to persuade, reading articles about smoking to gather information and participating in a debate. This is an ideal way of implementing literacy across the curriculum.

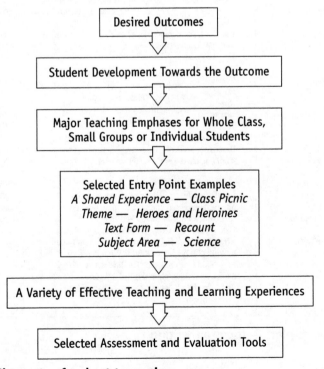

Figure 8.3: Elements of a short-term plan

*See CD-ROM for a range of Short-term Planning formats

Considerations for Short-term Planning

There is no single correct way to go about short-term planning. However, the following questions can be considered:

- What are students' needs, strengths and interests?
- What outcomes do I want students to be working towards?
- Which Major Teaching Emphases are going to be the focus of this planning period?
- What are my expectations?
- Is curriculum content being covered?
- Can I incorporate a topic from another subject area?
- What effective teaching and learning practices will I use?
- What learning experiences will students be involved in?
- What resources do I need to support these learning experiences?
- What texts, multimedia and human resources do I need to organise?
- What data will I collect to provide information about students' development?
- Will I share any information and with whom?

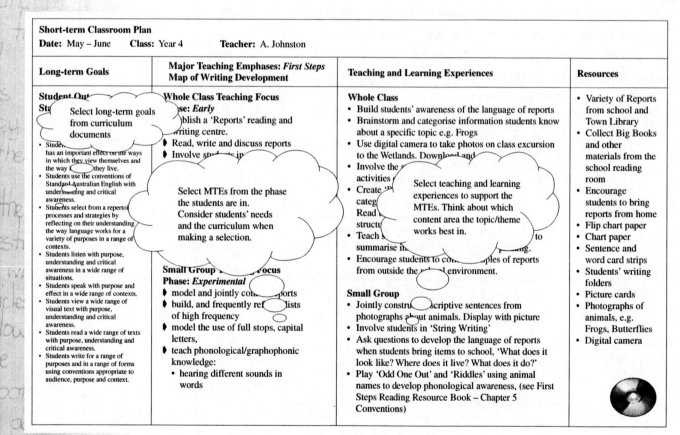

Figure 8.4: Short-term plan — focus on writing

Weekly or Daily Planning

This documentation is often described as the 'daily work pad', though it is usually prepared for a week in advance rather than day by day. In this document the specific plan of action for each lesson is written in sufficient detail to enable the teacher to organise resources and teach confidently.

While all teachers are aware there is no 'typical' school day, effective teachers find there is a need for planned organisation for their week and day with enough flexibility to deviate from routines. It is important that there is a balance of:

• explicit teacher instruction and independent student activity
• working as a whole class, in small groups and as individuals
• effective teaching and learning practices.

Some school systems have a recommended time allocation for each subject in the curriculum. The timetable can address such allocations by indicating separate sessions or showing a large, daily block of time that allows for the integration of numerous subjects, such as the various strands of literacy.

Year 3: Term 1 Timetable					
Time	**Monday**	**Tuesday**	**Wednesday**	**Thursday**	**Friday**
8:45	Reflection and Goal-setting	Fitness	Fitness	Fitness	Assembly
	Maths	Maths	Maths	Maths	Literacy
BREAK					
10:50	Literacy	Literacy	Literacy	Literacy	Maths
					Technology and Enterprise
LUNCH					
1:00	USSR	USSR	Library	USSR	USSR
	Phys Ed	Health	Drama	Society and Environment	Choir
	Japanese	Science	Music	Art	Sport
3:00	Literature				

Figure 8.5: A weekly timetable for Year 3

Planning the structure of the day is an important step. Teachers need to organise the day so it flows. Students need to see the connections between what they have learnt in a 'writing' session (for example) and how they can apply this knowledge in other curriculum areas. Teachers should also consider a mix of differently paced sessions that will help students reflect and re-engage with each task.

In the learning program there needs to be a balance of teacher-designed activities and blocks of time for students to pursue their own interests. Ensure that students have opportunities to use literacy for their own authentic and meaningful purposes.

Teachers need to encourage students to take responsibility for what they are learning. If they have taken part in negotiating what they are to learn, or have set their own daily or weekly goals, students feel they have some control over their learning. When students make decisions about what they will read or write or how they will respond to an oral or written text they are able to develop a sense of ownership that is vital if they are to become engaged in learning. Each student needs to see the purpose of their learning and how it applies to their daily lives.

Planning on a weekly or daily basis helps to ensure that the needs of individuals and small groups are met. If the students have difficulty with a concept or strategy one day, then the teacher can plan to repeat the teaching the next day, possibly using a different piece of text.

For example, during Modelled Reading a teacher had modelled the use of question marks, using a Big Book. It was evident during the session that students did not have a clear understanding of the use of question marks. The teacher adjusted the daily plan and the following day re-modelled the use of question marks with a new text. The students' needs continued to drive the planning for the following days.

Section of a Daily Work Plan: Year 6

Major Teaching Emphases: Read, write and discuss a range of text forms (historical recounts), focusing on purpose, audience, text structure and language features

	Monday	Tuesday	Wednesday	Thursday	Friday
11.00 – 12.00	**Objective:** Identify purpose and audience of a historical recount.	**Objective:** Identify the use of the past tense in historical recounts.	**Objective:** Identify main events of a historical recount.	**Objective:** Identify time connectives of a historical recount.	**Objective:** Identify the framework of a historical recount.
	Whole-class activities • Brainstorm what students already know about recount writing. • Shared reading of historical recount – 'Memories' by Mem Fox. • Discuss purpose of historical recounts.	**Whole-class activities** • Brainstorm what students know about gold being discovered in Australia. Group information (card cluster). • Shared reading of text 'Gold Discoveries in Australia'. • Discuss purpose and audience. Who would be the audience?	**Whole-class activities** • Brainstorm what students know about Jacques Cousteau. • Shared reading of text 'Cousteau: An Unauthorised Biography'. • Discuss 'main events'.	**Whole-class activities** • Modelled reading of recount – 'Ned Kelly'. • Type section of text from 'Ned Kelly' onto OH. Use an OH pen to mark words in the text that are time connectives and linking words. Begin class chart of time connectives and linking words.	**Whole-class activities** • Revisit text – 'Memories' by Mem Fox. Use the text as a model to elicit the structure of the text. Use labels to attach to each part of the text. Discuss the purpose of each part of the text.
	Small-group activities Group 1 (with teacher) Use small copies of 'Memories'. Answer explicit questions. Model how to find the key word in the text that leads to the answer. Group 2 (Ind) – Use Mem Fox website. Complete a retrieval chart by selecting information to fit under given headings.	**Small-group activities** Group 1 (Ind) – Make a list of things in the text (from print and visuals) that were used then but not used now. Group 2 (with teacher) Look at the language features that indicate something happened in the past.	**Small-group activities** • In pairs, list the main events in the recount • Choose 5 main events and put in sequence. **Whole-class activity** Show how events can be recorded as a timeline. Have pairs record their events as timelines.	**Small-group activity** Divide class into 3 groups (random selection). Give students one of the 3 books studied earlier in the week. Working as individual or pairs, make a list of the time connectives and linking words in their books.	**Small-group activities** • Give out copies of a printed historical recount and students work in small, heterogeneous groups to attach labels to each part of the text. • Using the labels the students have generated, create a class framework for a historical recount. • Give students an envelope containing a cut-apart recount and have them use the framework to put the text together again.
	Whole-class sharing In groups of 3, list 3 explicit bits of information found in reading the selection. Relate back to purpose of a historical recount.	**Whole-class sharing** As a whole class, share the information on how authors indicate something happened in the past. Begin class list of language features and visuals.	**Whole-class sharing** In groups of 4, share the main events chosen – justify choice.	**Whole-class sharing** Add time words to class chart.	**Whole-class sharing** Re-form the class and discuss the framework. Refine the framework as needed.

Figure 8.6: Section of a daily work plan — focus on literacy

Planning for Individuals

There may be occasions when the needs of particular students are not being met by the program provided. Students who are gifted or who have a learning disability may need a specific individual plan written for them. For plans to be truly responsive to the individual's needs often a team consisting of the teacher, parents, the student and other support services may need to be involved.

Knowing how the student is currently performing in school will help those involved in the planning team address areas where the student has an identified educational need. The plan needs to define the goals for a predetermined period, the actions and services needed to help the student, and a method of evaluating the student's progress.

The plan created is a working document that is flexible enough to respond to the changing needs of the student. The plan may be implemented for a specified length of time or until the outcomes are achieved. It may be implemented for a particular period of each school day such as the reading lesson or the literacy block. This allows the student to continue working with the rest of the class for the remainder of the day. The individual plan should be reviewed at regular intervals to ensure the most appropriate support is provided at all times.

Plans for Individual Students

Individual Education Plan – Literacy

Name: _George_   Date: _March_   Teacher: _____

Current First Steps phases:
Reading   _Early_
Writing   _____
Speaking and Listening   _____
Viewing   _____

Strengths	Student's Strategies to be developed

• *Talks about favourite books*
 • *Wants to get better at reading*
 • *has some strategies for solving unknown words*
   predicts using initial letters
   segments words
	predicting using text organisation cues (pictures and context)
	 re-reading when meaning is lost
	
	 Major Teaching Emphases
	 • *Continue to build student's knowledge base of cues - text structure and organisation*
	 • *Consolidate known comprehension strategies - predicting and connecting*
	 • *Model word solving strategies reading on and re-reading*
	 • *Model self reflection of strategies*
	 • *Continue to build student's sight vocabulary*
	 • *Teach student to identify explicit an implicit information and ideas*

Planned Activities and Experiences

Whole Class	Small Group	Individual	Notes
Modelled and Shared Reading *Making Predictions* *Personal Predictions* *Think-Pair-Share* *Think Sheets - complete working in pairs* *Picture Flick* *Connecting to the text* *Continue to encourage students to make self to text connections* *Model and discuss word solving strategies - reading on, re-reading, using context* *Develop class list of strategies* *Build students' sight vocabulary - brainstorm topic/theme words* *teach selection critical words prior to reading*	*Guided reading teach prediction and substantiation f* *Small group and partner co-operative cloze* *underline words in context students explain meaning* *Model how to identify context clues - looking for signal words in informational texts* *Silent reading and retelling* *Silent reading followed by reflection and sharing of strategies*	*Cloze activities focusing on: casting back over the text* *searching forward checking text organisation (pictures, headings)* *Oral cloze* *Written cloze* *Reflection journal - What did I learn? How did I learn it?* *Develop negotiated short term reading goals* *Model how to identify explicit information in a text. Underline explicit information* *Discuss what readers need to know to understand the text (implicit information)*	

Literacy Intervention Plan
Term One
2002

Year: Four
Student/s:

Date	Outcome/Target	Teaching Emphasis	Strategies	Classroom Management	Progress/Evidence
	• Develop a bank of sight words.	• Select high frequency words from writing to add to personal dictionary • Model strategies for learning new words.	• Use a personal dictionary • Make environmental print obvious • Use magnetic letters for Look, Cover, Write, Check • Modelled writing Shared reading	Independent Independent + small group Whole class	
	• Sounds out and represents all substantial sounds in words.	• Model representing sounds heard with common/basic letter patterns.	• Use magnetic letters • letter cards to play 'What Comes Next' • Coop Role - Code Breaker role - search for words with some initial letter/sound & search for personal words (recognition of sight words).	Independent + small grp Independent	
	• Uses basic sentence structure and some punctuation.	• Model creating sentences. Talk about letters & words, sentences.	• Use word cards/ punctuation cards to make sentences. • Practise re-reading. • Modelled writing	Independent & small group Whole class	

Figures 8.7a and b: Plans for individual students — focus on literacy (courtesy of Shannon Pearce, Australia)

Planning Across the Strands

Planning across the strands of literacy allows the content and strategies that will be taught to be integrated across the whole literacy block. For example, linking reading and writing together can allow students to read and research a topic during reading and use this information to write a report during writing.

One challenge for teachers in literacy planning is to ensure that students experience a balance of all four strands. Many teachers try to integrate the strands in an attempt to make learning more meaningful and at the same time to relieve some of the pressures of time.

Integrating Two Strands of Literacy

Strand/s: _____ Reading and Writing _____ Class _____ Year 6 (10/11 year olds) _____ Teacher _____ Planning Period _____

Focus: Novel — Charlotte's Web

Major Teaching Emphases		Whole Class Activities	Assessment
Whole Class: ____ Trans ____ Phase **Strand: Reading** Environment and Attitude • Foster students enjoyment of reading Use of Texts • Continue to teach students to analyse texts and identify explicit and implicit information and ideas Contextual Understanding • Discuss how readers may react to and interpret text differently depending on their background knowledge • Discuss how authors and illustrators have used devices to target specific audiences Conventions • Continue to build students sight vocabulary • Teach students to identify the role of language features in a variety of texts (literary) Process and Strategies • continue to build students knowledge base of cues (world knowledge) • consolidate known comprehension strategies and model additional strategies	____ Trans ____ Phase **Strand: Writing** Environment and Attitude • Foster students enjoyment of writing Use of Texts • Continue to read, write and discuss a range of text forms focussing on language features and text organisation Contextual Understanding • Jointly analyse how writers convey meaning for different purposes and audiences Conventions • Continue to involve students in constructing and manipulating sentences to enhance meaning • Continue to enrich students vocabulary Process and Strategies • Teach students to independently use a range of planning and organising strategies • Continue to develop students use of spelling strategies	• Select words from the novel and have students predict the story line. Share and record predictions. • Provide opportunities for students to read the novel. • As a whole class, introduce book discussion groups. (See First Steps Reading Resource Book – chapter 2 for procedure.) Establish book discussion groups and introduce the roles of the members. Initially give students role sheets to help them identify what the roles entail. Provide students with sticky notes and teach how to use these for discussing the story. • Use pages 122 and 123 of the novel and have students complete a Reader's Theatre. • At the end of the Reader's Theatre students select a character from the script and conduct an interview of that character. • Have students answer questions at the conclusion of several chapters. Include a range of literal, inferential and evaluative questions. Also have students list some questions they have for the author. • Have students complete a "Stop, Think, Feel, Share" at various points in the story. • Begin an interesting/difficult/unusual words chart identifying words from the story e.g. hullabaloo, salutations, pummelled, buffeted etc. • Use the collected words to create word clines, word sorts and other word level activities. • Comprehension strategies – connecting – discuss how readers make connection to the text to create meaning, sensory imaging – create drawings of parts of the book, discuss the images evoked. (See Knee and Harvey) • Build knowledge cues – farming, raising animals for meat. Look at issues from different points of view – rural/city, allocate students different roles – farmer, butcher, cook, environmentalist, vegetarian etc. • Have students begin a reflective journal where they enter – questions, comments or confusions. • Have students retell a chapter of the book. (See Cambourne) • Use a Plot Profile to list and rate events in a chapter/story. Discuss the organisation of the text – orientation, problem/resolution, ending and relate to chapters and to the text as a whole. • Use Charlotte's quote from chapter 12 – as a springboard for investigating the media. Students choose an article from the local paper to analyse the use of language. Discuss target audience and how language is used for the audience. • Use the argument between Wilbur and Templeton in Chapter 21 as a springboard for writing a narrative. Create an argument as the conflict of a narrative and then work forward and backward to create the context. (Major writing task)	• Collect role sheets and analyse written comments. • Assess Readers Theatre – interpretation of the text. • Collect Major writing task and assess using the narrative writing rubric. • Student self-assessment – reading strategies, logs. • Fluency checklist • Record or question and answer sessions (from guided reading) *Reading Procedures to be included* Modelled Reading Guided Reading Book Discussion Groups Independent Reading Reading Conferences *Teaching and Learning Practices to be included* Familiarising, Transforming Reflecting, Modelling, Sharing, Guiding, Analysing Practising, Applying

Major Teaching Emphasis	Major Teaching Emphasis	Small Group Activities	Resources
Small Group: Early Reading Phase • Familiarise students with the devices authors and illustrators use to influence the construction of meaning. • Teach students to identify explicit and implicit information • Model word solving strategies such as reading on and rereading	Small Group: Early Writing Phase • Encourage students to consider the need of the reader • Involve students in sentence manipulation – expanding and reducing sentences • Continue to build word banks – interesting words • Teach a range of spelling strategies – focus on visual patterns • Continue to build graphophonic knowledge – same sound can be represented by different letters.	These students will participate in many of the whole class activities listed above but will also have additional time and the following activities to cater for individual needs. • Involve students in small group guided reading sessions using a variety of books. • In small groups, conduct 'Reciprocal Reading' sessions focussing on the reading strategies of predicting, clarifying, summarising, questioning. Ensure students are given an opportunity to answer a variety of questions (literal, inferential, evaluative etc.) • Involve the students in word sorting – same sound different letters – create cumulative chart of patterns found. • Select sentences from text and students writing and use as basis for expanding and reducing. Involve student in physical sentence manipulation. • Scaffold writing tasks by providing a framework from which to plan.	Charlotte's Web – White First Steps Map of Development Book First Steps Reading Resource Book Revisit Reflect and Retell – Hoyt Reading Reminders – Burke Novel Workshop 1 – Pyne Mosaic of Thought – Knee Strategies that Work – Harvey Literature Circles – Harvey Read and retell – Cambourne

Figure 8.8

Integrating Four Strands of Literacy

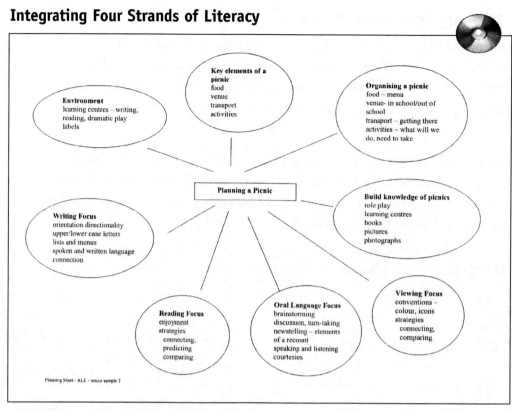

Environment
learning centres – writing, reading, dramatic play labels

Key elements of a picnic
food
venue
transport
activities

Organising a picnic
food – menu
venue- in school/out of school
transport – getting there
activities – what will we do, need to take

Planning a Picnic

Build knowledge of picnics
role play
learning centres
books
pictures
photographs

Writing Focus
orientation directionality
upper/lower case letters
lists and menus
spoken and written language connection

Reading Focus
enjoyment
strategies
   connecting,
   predicting
   comparing

Oral Language Focus
brainstorming
discussion, turn-taking
newstelling – elements of a recount
speaking and listening courtesies

Viewing Focus
conventions –
   colour, icons
strategies
   connecting,
   comparing

Planning Sheet - ALE - junior sample 2

Figure 8.9

Organisational Structures for Individual Lessons

The level of documentation for each lesson will vary from teacher to teacher. Teachers may carry much of the finer detail in their heads or have set routines that have been documented in the long-term plan and used on a regular basis. Effective lessons are:
• tailored for a specific group of students
• adapted to meet a range of student needs and abilities
• designed to involve all students in purposeful activities.

Grouping Considerations

A comprehensive approach to teaching literacy needs to ensure that throughout the course of the day and week, students have the opportunity to work with different peers in a range of different-sized groups. It is important to provide opportunities to learn literacy as part of the whole-class group as well as in small groups, with partners or on an individual basis.

Whole Class

During these sessions a shared context is created. Explicit teaching, class sharing or development of a learning community may take place.

Small Groups or Pairs

Cooperative and flexible small groups and partner work allow explicit teaching to occur that effectively meets the needs of all students. These groupings assist students to develop collaborative learning behaviours.

Individual

Students need opportunities to take responsibility for their own learning by working independently on self-selected or teacher-directed tasks. This time allows teachers to monitor individual progress and provide additional support as needed.

The greatest challenge for teachers is to design a model that will allow them to plan and manage a balance of whole-class, small-group and individual teaching and learning experiences. There is no single organisational model that will provide the perfect balance for all students. It is therefore important for teachers to examine different suggestions for organising groups during the literacy time, and adapt structures to meet their particular needs. The organisational structure that is suitable for a particular day may be changed the following day due to differing needs.

Some ways of organising the class groupings are as follows:

X X X X X X X X X X X X X X X X X X X X X X X X (T) Teacher works with whole class.	X X X X X X X X X X X X (T) X X X X X X X X X X X X Teacher works with small group, while rest of class works independently.	X X X X X X X X X X X X (T) X X X X X X X X X X Students work in pairs. X X Teacher moves among pairs, X X helping as needed.
X X X X X X X X X X X X X X X X X X X X X (T) X X X Students work in groups. Teacher works with one group or rotates around groups.	X X X X X X X X X X X X X X X X X X X X (T) X X X X Students work individually. Teacher works with individuals.	X X X X X X X X X X X X X X X X X X X (T) X X X X X Teacher works with most of the class while a small group works together independently.

Figure 8.10: Class groupings

Flexible Grouping

It is important that grouping is flexible and that all students are exposed to different language models, interests of other students and varied social situations. Flexible grouping allows students to work in different kinds of groups depending on the intended learning outcome. For example, all students who are in the same phase on a *First Steps* Map of Development might be grouped together to work on a particular strategy. Once that strategy has been learnt the group dissolves. Teachers need to:

• plan how the groups are going to be set up

• decide what size groups would be most appropriate for the particular activity

• decide how long students will stay in an assigned group.

The following table (Figure 8.11) lists some of the ways in which groups may be formed. Teachers need to decide on the learning objective for the session and select the most appropriate grouping to achieve that objective.

Different Ways of Grouping Students

Grouping Based on ...	How to Organise	Used when ...	Example
Ability	Students who perform similarly on certain tasks are put into the same group.	Teachers want students to work on a task at their instructional level.	Guided Reading lesson
Learning Style	Select students who have the same learning style.	Teachers want students to benefit from working with peers who learn the same way as they do.	Students choose how to best represent their learning, e.g. perhaps to draw, perhaps to dramatise.
Interest or Motivation	Conduct an interest survey. Students who have expressed an interest in a particular topic are grouped together.	Teachers want to capture the interest and motivation that students have expressed.	Research on an item of interest
Knowledge of Subject	Students who have knowledge about a particular subject are grouped together.	Teachers want to: • build on and consolidate students' understanding of a topic • observe how similar interests can unite diverse students.	• Research project • Writing a report on a chosen theme
Common Needs	Based on a needs analysis.	Teachers want to teach a particular skill or strategy for reinforcement, consolidation or enrichment.	Introduction to proof-reading or a particular spelling strategy
Social (cooperative) Factors	Selection of certain students so they can team up or cooperate on the basis of work habits or behaviour.	Teachers want to develop cooperative learning skills and get students to work together towards a common goal.	• Produce a class newsletter • Make a Big Book
Student Choice	Based on the wish of certain students to work together.	Teachers want to capture students' interests and preparedness to work cooperatively.	• Reading the same book • Writing a group report
Random Selection	Have each student's name in a hat. Select from the hat to form small groups.	Teachers want different students to experience working together.	• News-telling • Interviews • Think–Pair–Share • Readers' Theatre

Figure 8.11: Adapted from Opitz, M. 1998

Lesson Structures

When teachers are planning for individual lessons they need to take into consideration the grouping arrangements that best meet the needs of students.

The structure and grouping within each lesson will also vary depending upon the purpose. A lesson often includes whole-class, small-group and/or individual activities followed by whole-class reporting and reflecting.

There are countless variations in group sizes and grouping arrangements to achieve specific ends. The following examples illustrate five ways in which literacy lessons could be structured.

Example 1

In this organisational structure, following the whole-class session, most of the class works on a related activity. The teacher works with a small group who have been identified because of a common need.

Whole Class
Whole-class session to introduce a particular skill, strategy or understanding, e.g. Modelled Reading.

Group selection is based on a common need.

Activity
Majority of the class works in small groups, in pairs or individually on activities related to the whole-class experience, e.g. comprehension strategy practice.

Small Group
Small group is withdrawn by teacher to work on a specific skill, using the whole-class activity as a base, e.g. Guided Reading.

Whole Class
Whole class reports and reflects on their learning, e.g. Think–Pair–Share (see Chapter 9).

Example 2

In this organisational structure the whole-class session is followed by the formation of small groups.

Whole Class
Whole-class session to introduce a particular skill, strategy or understanding, e.g. Shared Writing.

Group selection can be social, by student choice or random.

| **Activity** Students work in a small group to complete a shared task. | **Activity** Students work in a small group to complete a shared task. | **Activity** Students work in a small group to complete a shared task. | **Activity** Students work in a small group to complete a shared task. |

Each group works on the same activity (e.g. identifying key words and phrases) using different content.

Whole Class
Whole class reports and reflects on their learning, e.g. **Envoy** (see Chapter 9).

Example 3

This organisational structure is appropriate when all students in the class need to access the same piece of text. Each set activity allows students to access the text at different levels, but when students report and reflect they have gathered similar information. It is an organisational structure that can easily be carried over to curriculum content areas where students may be working from a textbook.

Whole Class
Whole-class session to introduce a topic and make connections to prior knowledge, e.g. brainstorming.

All students are then presented with the same piece of text about the topic.

Group selection is based on ability.

Activity
Students work in small groups, in pairs or individually to read the text and create a summary of the key points.

Activity
Students work in small groups, in pairs or individually to read the text and complete a modified activity.

Activity
Students work in small groups, in pairs or individually to read the text and complete a modified activity.

The teacher is free to move among the groups and provide help where needed.

Whole Class
Whole class reports and reflects on their learning, e.g. **Jigsaw** (see Chapter 9).

Example 4

In this organisational structure the class works in three groups. The teacher works with one group during the session while the other two groups work independently on a set activity or at a learning centre.

This structure is likely to be repeated for three days so the teacher has the opportunity to work specifically with each group.

Whole Class
Whole-class session to introduce a particular skill, strategy or understanding, e.g. Shared Viewing.

Group selection is based on ability or common need.

Small Group
Small group is withdrawn by teacher to work on a specific skill, using the whole-class activity as a base, e.g. Guided Viewing.

Activity
Students work in small groups, in pairs or individually to complete an activity related to the whole-class session, e.g. searching websites for information.

Activity
Students work in small groups, in pairs, or individually on a learning-centre activity.

Whole Class
Whole class reports and reflects on their learning, e.g. Show and Tell.

Example 5

In this organisational structure, when the whole-class session finishes, each student works independently on an activity related to the whole-class experience.

> **Whole Class**
> Whole-class session to introduce a particular skill, strategy or understanding, e.g. making connections.

> Students work independently on the same activity related to whole-class experience.

Once the students are working independently the teacher is free to:
- conduct conferences with individual students
- identify a particular group of students who need assistance and work with them.

> **Whole Class**
> Whole class reports and reflects on their learning, e.g. individual volunteers share.

Working with Groups

Group Management

The ideal classroom has students organised in a variety of grouping arrangements so all needs are being met. However, working with one group of students is not productive if the remainder of the class is constantly interrupting and calling for the teacher's attention. It is essential that all students know how to work independently and what procedures to follow when the teacher is busy with another group. It is well worthwhile spending time at the beginning of every school year teaching students the procedures that are to be adopted. Brainstorm with the class what they can do to avoid interrupting the teacher and the focus group. Create a class chart that reminds students of their options.

When I Need Help I Can:
- ask the nominated person at my table
- skip that question or word and try the next one.

When I Finish Work Early I Can:
- check back through my work
- read a book
- work at a learning centre (no more than four people at a time).

It is advisable to begin the year with the class working as a whole so there is time for students to become accustomed to general classroom procedures. It also allows time for the teacher to become more aware of students' capabilities and needs. Start small when organising groups.

A possible transition towards successfully using small-group work is described below.

The teacher:
- works with the majority of the class while a few students work independently
- works with the majority of the class while some students work with partners
- works with the majority of the class while one small group works together independently
- works with the majority of the class while two small groups work independently
- decides where explicit teaching or support is needed while multiple groups work independently.

There is no nominated time frame within which this will occur; it may take weeks or even months, but the time spent reaching this end will be worthwhile.

As well as being able to work independently, students will need to learn the strategies to enable them to work cooperatively in a variety of group situations. Learning to cooperate is a long-term process. Teachers need to take time to explicitly teach the cooperative strategies, and to provide time and opportunities for students to practise and receive feedback. They can implement group-management strategies to encourage cooperation.

Assigning Roles

Teachers may assign roles to individual students to facilitate the participation of all group members and to help structure the actual discussion. There is a range of roles that could be assigned.
- Recorder — records group decisions, asks questions to clarify what people mean
- Reporter — reports the ideas and decisions to the class
- Encourager — makes sure everyone is participating, offers praise and encouragement
- Manager — collects any resources that are needed, explains and clarifies the task, summarises where the group is up to, has contact with the teacher if needed.

Each role needs to be introduced by:
- showing the role in operation; for example, using role-play or 'fish bowl' strategy (see Glossary)
- building a Y- or T-chart about what the role 'sounds like', 'looks like' and 'feels like' (see Chapter 9)
- providing opportunities to practise.

Students in group discussion wear name tags to identify the roles recorder, encourager, manager and reporter.

Numbering Off

Students in the group count off to identify the order in which they will speak. This works especially well when students are making lists; e.g. a list of questions, a list of possible solutions. Numbering Off eliminates the difficulty of deciding who goes first or last.

Structuring Responses

Each group member is given the opportunity to make one comment or ask one question in response to the opening statement of the other group members. For example, member 1 makes a statement — members 2, 3 and 4 respond; member 2 makes a statement — members 1, 3 and 4 respond, and so on.

Key Communicator

If the group comes to a problem and needs to speak to the teacher, only the designated person is permitted to call for the teacher's attention and seek help.

Effective group management in any classroom is a long-term process, not a one-off event. Teachers will develop their own approach to group organisation and management within the classroom and will use methods that work successfully for them and their students. Methods and approaches may need to be altered each year.

CHAPTER 9

The Metacognitive Process: Reflecting, Representing and Reporting

Learning how to learn — that is, developing a repertoire of thinking processes and strategies which can be applied to solve problems — is a major goal of literacy education. The challenge for educators in the information age is to teach students strategies that will not become obsolete. The metacognitive process empowers students to be aware of themselves as learners and to control and improve their own literacy. Those teachers who teach students the use of this process promote learning.

Metacognitive thinking is an interwoven process of:
- reflecting (thinking back over the strategies used or the content learnt)
- representing (demonstrating the learning)
- reporting (sharing information with others).

Metacognitive thinking is pivotal to the *First Steps* resource. It is through this process that students are able to make their learning meaningful. The process of metacognition can be modelled and introduced as early as Kindergarten and Pre-primary.

Supporting Metacognitive Thinking

The effectiveness of metacognitive thinking and practice depends upon a number of contributing factors. Teachers can strive to:
- create a positive classroom climate that encourages acceptance, tolerance, risk-taking, and an awareness of thinking
- organise the classroom environment to facilitate metacognitve thinking; e.g. provide opportunities for students to work independently and in small groups
- ensure administrative support and school-wide commitment so metacognitive thinking receives status, and time is allowed for students to employ, practise and refine the strategies
- ensure that whole-school structures and ethos are in place to

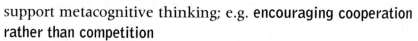

support metacognitive thinking; e.g. **encouraging cooperation rather than competition**
- assist students to develop a metacognitive thinking vocabulary of terms such as 'strategy', 'goal', 'reflect'
- establish and share goals (both process and content) before lessons begin. The extent to which these goals have been achieved forms the basis of the reflection
- provide specific, positive and corrective feedback on strategy use or evidence of metacognitive thinking skills being employed
- provide meaningful content for reflection by integrating the teaching of metacognitive thinking with all areas of the curriculum
- model metacognitive strategies so students get insights into how and why these are applied
- teach the skills and strategies necessary for students to work cooperatively
- cater for different learning styles by encouraging students to represent their learning in a variety of ways.

Students need to:
- be encouraged to take responsibility for, and ownership of their own learning
- be encouraged to participate in class decision-making sessions; e.g. **brainstorming, class meetings, group work**
- be provided with clear expectations
- be allowed opportunity and time to practise and develop metacognitive thinking strategies in meaningful contexts
- develop independent work habits
- have a range of strategies to apply when they encounter difficulties.

Teaching Metacognitive Thinking

If students are able to select a strategy that is most appropriate for a task, monitor their thinking and evaluate the effectiveness of their strategies at the completion of the task, they are being metacognitive.

For this to occur, teachers will need to teach students what is involved in being metacognitive.
- The process of metacognitive thinking will need to be modelled many times. This will be more successful if teachers focus on one or two aspects of the process at a time and over a series of lessons. As part of modelling, it is important that teachers explain not only how strategies are used but also why particular strategies are useful or appropriate.

- The students will need opportunities to practise metacognitive thinking in many contexts. As part of a reflection session at the end of a lesson, for instance, teachers can ask students which strategies they used, how successful the strategies were and what they could try next time.
- The teacher will need to provide students with explicit feedback and acknowledgement of their attempts to be metacognitive; e.g. by asking targeted questions.

Teacher:	Kim, I noticed you were reading-on in Guided Reading today. Why did you choose to use that strategy?
Kim:	*Well, I came to a couple of words that I didn't know, and I wanted to see if there were any clues in the rest of the sentence to help me.*
Teacher:	Did that strategy work for you?
Kim:	*Well, it helped me with one of the words but not with this one (points to 'oasis').*
Teacher:	Can you think of anything else you could have done?
Kim:	*I tried to sound it out, but that didn't help either.*
Teacher:	Show me what you did?
Kim:	*oa—s—i—s.*
Teacher:	Mmm, I see. Do you remember in our discussion before we began reading, we talked about the deserts of the Sahara, and Paul mentioned the special name we give to places in the desert where water is found?
Kim:	*Oh, that's right, an oasis. Mmm ... if I had tried using the letter names of the 'o' and 'a' it might have helped.*
Teacher:	Yes, that might work. Or you could remember some of the words we discussed before reading and make a prediction about which one it was likely to be.

Figure 9.1: Transcript of teacher providing explicit feedback

By reflecting on learning in this manner, teachers are encouraging students to be aware that strategies can be applied in many situations. As part of the metacognitive process, teachers can give students an opportunity to think about how particular strategies can be applied across other learning areas. In this way, teachers are not just equipping students for school; they are equipping them with life skills they can apply in other learning situations.

Metacognitive Thinking Vocabulary

Students need to understand the meaning of certain terminology such as the following, and be able to use it in context.

Terms	Definitions
articulate	being able to describe what is being done
feedback	information given to a learner to direct, improve or control future learning
goal	some point towards which one strives, a target, as in 'My reading goal is to read three chapter books in six weeks'
effective	successful, something that worked well
ineffective	not successful, something that didn't work well
negotiate	to reach agreement through discussion and consensus
reflect	to think back over a learning experience, task or product to ascertain its effectiveness or otherwise
report	to share information with others
represent	to demonstrate learning
self-assessment	making judgements about one's progress and/or achievement
self-talk	asking questions or making comments to oneself, verbally or internally
strategy	a plan of attack, knowing what to do and when to do it
successful	accomplishing what was intended

Figure 9.2

The Metacognitive Process

This process consists of three interwoven aspects — reflecting, representing and reporting.

Reflecting on the Learning

Reflecting involves analysing and making judgements about what has been learnt and how learning took place. For this to be successful, students need the opportunity and structures to allow them to stand back and think of what they have learnt. It is through reflection in literacy, for instance, that explicit understandings about textual, grammatical, phonological and spelling systems can be refined.

Reflecting enables students to:
- become aware of the processes and strategies they are using
- monitor the use of their processes and strategies
- take control of how, when, why and to what extent those processes and strategies are applied
- refine their processes and strategies
- critically evaluate the success of their processes and strategies.

Representing the Learning

Representing thinking in concrete and active forms helps students to externalise and generalise their thoughts. Representing can be a means of learning as it helps students come to grips with new information and/or learning.

Following on from the reflection process, it is often helpful if the teacher demonstrates how to make thinking concrete by writing a key word or two, drawing a picture, or constructing a simple graphic such as a flow chart or Venn diagram. Students then need to be given opportunities to represent their learning in a way that is meaningful to them.

Catering for Different Learning Styles

It needs to be remembered that students in the class have many different learning styles and there is no single way of representing learning appropriate for all learners. Students can be shown various representations to enable them to choose the one that is most appropriate for their learning style and the task at hand. Students need to become aware of their own learning style or preferences. It is important to provide opportunities to discuss why one representation is more effective than another and to explore others' styles or preferences. (See Figure 9.3.)

Representing Learning

Preferred Learning Style	May Prefer to Represent Learning Through:
Visual learners	• highlighting texts • creating pictures, diagrams, charts, videos or maps • writing notes in different colours
Auditory learners	• participating in group discussions • recording on an audio or videotape • putting their ideas to music
Kinaesthetic learners	• dramatising or acting out • building a model • devising a game to demonstrate a concept
Interactive learners	• completing group projects • peer tutoring • participating in group discussion
Print-oriented learners	• reading, printing and drawing • constructing story maps, flow charts or newspapers • devising questions at different levels; e.g. using Bloom's *Taxonomy*

Figure 9.3

Reporting the Learning

Students often clarify their thinking and understanding by talking. It is through reporting to others that students refine, consolidate and extend their learning. Students need the opportunity to work in a variety of groupings and to report on both learning processes and products. Reporting does not need to be a 'formal' presentation performed before the whole class at the end of every lesson. It can simply be turning to a partner and stating what strategy was used to spell a word in writing, or what was enjoyable or challenging about the activity just completed.

Sharing information

Showing a piece of work

Reflecting on and Representing Learning

There are many different ways students can be encouraged to reflect on and represent their learning. The type of activity chosen will depend on:

- the time available
- the time span; e.g. a single lesson or a whole unit of work
- students' familiarity with the activity
- the purpose
- the number of students involved; e.g. whole class, small group, partners
- the learning styles of students.

The activities listed under 'Five-minute Reflections' are probably more suited to reflection or representation sessions after a single lesson. They are brief but can still be highly effective. Other reflecting and representing activities may take longer and involve students reflecting on many aspects of their learning. These may be used at the end of a unit of work. It is acknowledged that students have different learning styles and while the activities listed may appear to be focused on writing, there is no reason why teachers could not vary the activities by having students complete them orally or using a visual representation; e.g. drawing or making a model.

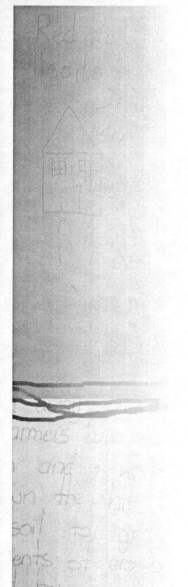

Strategies for Reflecting and Representing Learning

1 'Five-minute Reflections'
2 Goal-setting
3 Self-questioning
4 Think–Pair–Share
5 Reflective Questionnaire
6 Cumulative Charts
7 Learning Charts
8 Concept Maps
9 Venn Diagrams
10 Learning Logs
11 Look What I Can Do
12 T-Charts
13 Y-Charts
14 KWHL Framework

1 'Five-minute Reflections'

- Give students a few minutes to think about something they have enjoyed or puzzled over during the day. Share with others.
- Use an aid such as a puppet. Let students tell the puppet about something enjoyable they have done or learnt during the lesson.
- Model the process of metacognitive thinking at least once a day. Modelling of the metacognitive process can include:
  – an attitudinal element; e.g. 'I did a good job at …'
  – strategies being used; e.g. 'I read to the end of the line'
  – knowledge and understandings; e.g. 'A full stop is used at the end of a sentence.'
- At the end of the day, encourage students to think about a special event or achievement at school that they can share with their family.
- Encourage students to get started with metacognitive thinking by answering simple questions such as:
  – Who did you work with?
  – What did you enjoy?
  – What was difficult?
  – What was easy?
  – What did you learn?
- During any lesson stop and ask students to think of a question that comes to mind. Have students put their question to the group or class. For example, during a reading task, stop at predetermined places and have students ask each other a question about the reading strategies being used.

- Have students keep a learning log or reflective journal. As a quick reflection, stop the lesson at strategic places and ask students to write in their journals. This may include questions they have about the text they are reading or writing, the strategies they are using or the way they are working.
- The teacher can ask a question about a specific aspect of learning. The group members then 'whip around' the circle with thirty seconds each to comment on the question. For example, the teacher may ask, 'What helped your group work successfully today?' Students in the group respond swiftly in turn. (Adapted from Hill, S. and T. 1990.)
- Students can use charts available in the classroom as a basis for reflection; e.g. a **T-Chart constructed on effective group work**.
- Encourage students to keep a very simple journal that consists of sketches, drawings, photographs, artefacts or words about aspects of their learning.

Figure 9.4: Text-to-self connection

- Introduce students to a number of different ways in which learning can be represented. Networks, branching tree structures, chains, pyramids and explosion charts are just some of the ways. These representations will need to be introduced and modelled over time in appropriate contexts.
- 'Thumbs Up, Thumbs Down': This activity can help both teacher and students reflect on how the lesson is progressing. At various points during the lesson the teacher can stop and ask, 'Who's with me?', 'Who understands?', 'Who's keeping up?'. Students give the thumbs up if the answer is 'yes' and thumbs down if 'no'. The teacher is able to see who needs help or whether to modify the pace of the lesson if it is progressing too quickly or going too slowly.

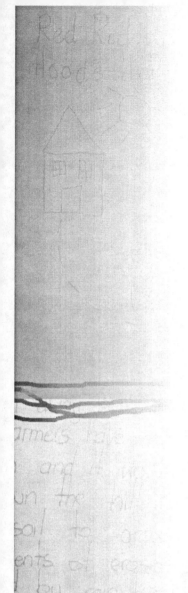

2 Goal-setting

Being able to set goals and reflect on whether they have been achieved or not can be very empowering for students.

To enable students to set and monitor appropriate learning goals teachers need to provide scaffolding and guidance in this process. The significant factor which underlies successful learning is the degree to which students have actually identified, adopted and reflected on their own goals for learning through problem-solving. Once the goals have been determined in this way, students can map the learning pathway and monitor their progress towards the achievement of the goals.

Teachers can assist this process by:
- modelling goal-setting in daily lessons,
- planning and implementing action plans to achieve the goal
- celebrating the achievement of goals.

Modelling Goal-setting

- When introducing students to goal-setting it is recommended that teachers work at the whole-class level before asking students to set small-group or individual goals. Teachers and students can work together to identify goals that will have benefits for all students in the class; e.g. **'Our class goal is to raise our hands when we want to talk to the teacher'**, **'Our goal is to help the teacher remember our names.'**
- Learning goals, while being aimed at the achievement of outcomes or major objectives in the long term, need to be formulated around specific skills or understandings that can be achieved over a short time span. When students are first introduced to goal-setting there can be a tendency to adopt 'motherhood statements' as goals. While these statements are highly desirable in their own right, they are difficult to achieve in the short term. Students need to understand that goals should be small, concrete, attainable and measurable. The statements from the 'Look What I Can Do' pages in the *First Steps* Maps of Development can provide some guidance for teachers as they help students to set goals.
- Teachers can begin the goal-setting process by modelling and discussing effective and ineffective goals before asking students to construct their own. A quick and easy way for the teacher to do this is to write on the chalkboard an effective or ineffective goal at the beginning of each lesson and discuss whether the goal is specific, achievable, and so on. When set in this way the goals can provide a focus for reflection at the end of the lesson; e.g. **'Let's look at the goal for the lesson. Did we achieve it?'**

Planning and Implementing Action Plans

- Encouraging students to record their goals is often useful. Students are able to reflect on and update their goals regularly and they can observe their progress.
- Clarifying a goal is often a lengthy tactic, but it is an important step in the process. One way of clarifying a goal is to articulate it for others, perhaps through Think–Pair–Share.
- To focus attention on the goal, the teacher and students can jointly construct criteria that make the goal explicit. Using these criteria, students are then able to assess their individual achievement towards the goal.

My Goal for Reading	
Goal: Use headings and subheadings to locate information in texts	Yes or No
I know that headings and subheadings are usually printed in a different, larger and bolder font.	
I know that underneath a heading or subheading I will find more detailed information about the topic.	
I can find chapter headings on a Contents page.	
I can use headings and subheadings in an Index.	
I can 'skim' headings and subheadings to gain an overview of the information in a chapter.	
I scan headings and subheadings to help me locate information I need.	
Have I achieved my goal?	

Figure 9.5: Negotiated criteria for selected goal

My Goal for Reading			
Goal: To retell the story of a picture book			
Name: _____	Always	Sometimes	Not yet
I can say where and when the story happens.			
I can give the names of the most important characters.			
I can describe these characters so others know lots about them.			
I can say what happens at the beginning of the story and what happens next.			
I can put things that happen in the story into the right order.			
I can say what happens at the end of the story.			
Did I achieve my goal?		Yes	Not yet
To improve my work I can:			

Figure 9.6: Negotiated criteria for selected goal

Celebrating the Achievement of the Goal

It is important that students and teachers recognise when goals have been achieved and celebrate that achievement. Using 'Two Stars and a Wish' is a good way of reflecting positively on the achievement of a goal and indicating a future direction (see Chapter 6).

3 Self-questioning

Careful self-questioning can help students reflect on and improve their learning. To assist students develop self-questioning the teacher will need to model the process of self-talk so students can see the relationship between the thinking and the plan of action.

For example, the teacher may begin by saying: 'I wonder if this would be the best way of …' or 'How can I find out this information?'. The teacher will also need to make explicit the reasons why one strategy was chosen over another. 'I think I will use "Have-a-Go" to spell this word because I'm not sure of the spelling of the "ee" sound in "achieve".'

Any one of the following questions can provide a useful starting point to develop students' self-questioning. These can be used for quick reflection at the end of a lesson or for a more considered reflection at the end of a unit or theme.

- How did I do that?
- What was I thinking when I did that?
- Why did I choose that strategy?
- Did I understand what I was doing?
- Was I able to work independently?
- Is there anything I still need to find out?
- Could I explain the steps I took?
- What would I do differently next time?

4 Think–Pair–Share

Think–Pair–Share allows students to think about a topic or issue, or reflect on learning and then share their thoughts with a partner. It therefore involves reflecting and reporting. Using Think–Pair–Share allows students to express their ideas in a non-threatening way and involves all students, not just the vocal few. Students can be paired with different partners to give them an opportunity to work with as many others as possible.

- Arrange students in pairs and explain the topic or issue to be discussed. It may also be necessary to revise appropriate speaking and listening behaviours at this point.
- Allow students some thinking time to process their information.

- Pairs sit closely, face each other and take turns sharing their ideas. The listener can question the speaker to avoid any confusion.
- Pairs may then contribute ideas to small groups or alternatively the teacher may select several students to share with the whole group.
- Ideas may be recorded in chart form depending on the purpose of the lesson.
- Have students review their roles as speaker and listener by offering each other positive or constructive feedback.

5 Reflective Questionnaire

A Reflective Questionnaire provides a framework for students to reflect on their learning. The questions can be varied to suit the students or the context.

- What are the main things you have learnt in this topic, unit or lesson?
- What helped you learn?
- How does what you learnt in this topic, unit or lesson relate to what happens in real life?

6 Cumulative Charts

A Cumulative Chart is a representation of the growing understandings of the whole class in specific areas. It is constructed as a direct result of the regular reporting of learning outcomes by individuals or small groups. The chart should be an evolving entity and never set in concrete. It can be amended or added to as strategies and knowledge are refined and recorded.

The Cumulative Chart can be used as:
- a highly focused record of learning that has occurred
- a reference point for all members of the class to use as they read and write
- a clear model of how small specific elements combine to form a cohesive structure or system; e.g. a spelling chart.

Cumulative Spelling Chart

How do I work out how to spell a new word?

— Does the word look right? If not, have I tried another way to write it?

— What does the word mean? Is it like any other words I know?

— Do I know where the word comes from?

— Can I find the part I'm not sure of and underline it?

— Have I tried to find the word in a word bank or a dictionary?

— Can I divide the word into parts? Have any parts been added to it?

— Can I divide the word into syllables?

— If I say the word slowly, can I hear the sounds in order?

Figure 9.7: A Cumulative Spelling Chart

7 Learning Charts

Learning Charts are another form of cumulative chart that can be used to represent and summarise reflections. The difference is that Learning Charts usually represent two sorts of learning: content and also processes and strategies. When students become confident in distinguishing between the two, the classifications can be used as an organising framework in their Learning Journals.

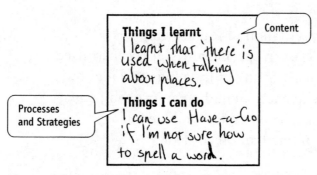

Content

Things I learnt
I learnt that 'there' is used when talking about places.

Processes and Strategies

Things I can do
I can use Have-a-Go if I'm not sure how to spell a word.

Figure 9.8: A student's Learning Chart

8 Concept Maps

Concept Maps diagrammatically represent what the learner knows about the links and relationships between concepts. Concept Maps organise, enhance and encourage understanding. They are sometimes called semantic webs, graphic organisers or mind maps. Concept mapping looks like clustering or brainstorming but goes one step further by stating the relationships between the ideas or concepts.

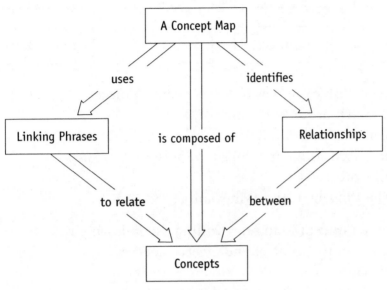

Figure 9.9: Based on 'Inspiration' — www.inspiration.com

Concept mapping is used most often to represent learning in content areas such as science or social studies. Concept Maps can:
• be used to activate or retrieve prior knowledge
• illustrate the links between existing and new knowledge
• encourage divergent and metacognitive thinking
• act as a diagnostic tool for teachers.

Constructing Concept Maps

Teachers need to model the process of constructing Concept Maps.
• Brainstorm ideas together. (It will make the next stage of construction easier if the words are written on cards or adhesive notes.)
• Ask the students to group the words. Each concept can only be used once so students will need to carefully consider the placement. Concepts are usually organised from general to specific.
• Draw lines or arrows between the concepts. Label the links between the concepts with words to describe the relationships that exist.

- Linking words or phrases can be used more than once within the same Concept Map. The following words and phrases may be useful.

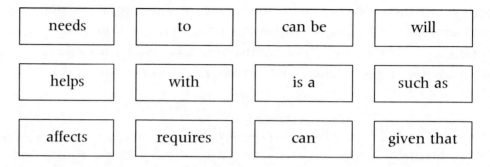

needs	to	can be	will
helps	with	is a	such as
affects	requires	can	given that

- If appropriate, link examples to the concepts. Connect these with the phrases 'such as' or 'for example'.
- For younger students with limited writing skills, Concept Maps can be introduced using drawings to represent some aspects rather than words.

(Adapted from Wilson, J. and Wing Jan, L. 1993.)

Figure 9.10 is a Concept Map representing the following Key Understandings on the topic of endangered species.
- People contribute to animals becoming extinct.
- There are other reasons for extinction.
- There are things people can do to help.

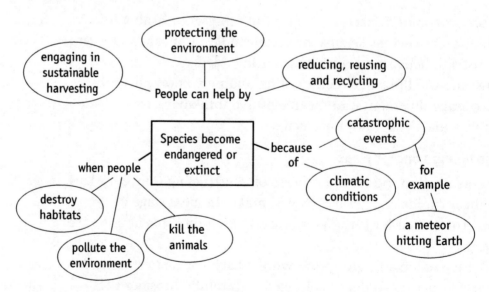

Figure 9.10: Concept Map

9 Venn Diagrams

Venn Diagrams are used to describe and compare characteristics and attributes of things, people, places, events or ideas. They are a useful tool for comparing what is similar and what is not.

When students first begin using Venn Diagrams have them compare and contrast two items only.

Example:

Teacher: 'Tell me about these words: *chick, cheese, chop, each, eat, tree.*'
Student: 'I drew a Venn Diagram showing that some of the words just have <u>ch</u>, some of the words had the <u>ee</u> sound, and <u>cheese</u> and <u>each</u> had both.'

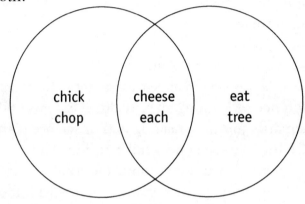

Figure 9.11: Venn Diagram comparing two attributes

As the students become more proficient with the use of Venn Diagrams more elements can be introduced.

Example:

Compare the princesses from the books *Princess Smartypants, The Balloon Tree* and *The Paperbag Princess*.

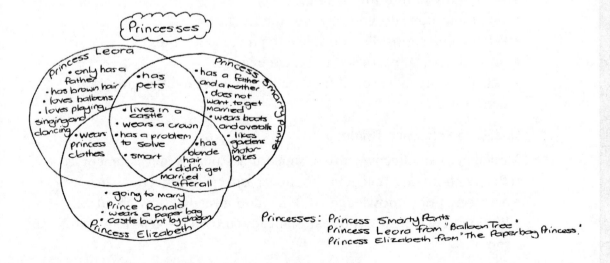

Figure 9.12: A student's comparison of three characters

10 Learning Logs

Learning Logs are journals in which students record their growing understandings about the content and processes of their learning. Learning Logs are most effective when they go beyond just a diary of the day's events. They should involve the students in identifying, analysing and reflecting on aspects of their learning. Compiling a Class Learning Log can be used to demonstrate the process.

Students benefit from the opportunity and support to think about:
- the extent to which they have achieved their goals or the goals of the lesson
- what new things they have learnt
- what they have enjoyed
- what has challenged them
- what they still don't understand
- what new things they want to find out.

The above criteria can be applied to all learning areas. Teachers can facilitate the transference of learning by providing students with, for example, mathematics journals, reading logs or science diaries. In order to minimise the overload on working memory it is recommended that students focus on keeping a journal in one learning area only. This enables them to come to terms with the purpose, format and entry styles of Learning Logs.

Teachers can use a range of ways to assist students' transition from simply recounting the day's activities to reflecting on the learning.

Providing Guiding Questions or Prompts

Suggestions:
- In spelling/maths/reading today I learnt ...
- What did you find interesting?
- What questions do you have for the teacher?
- What connections did you make to previous learning?
- In spelling/reading I used the ... strategy.
- Was the strategy successful? What could you do differently next time?

Modelling Reflective Thinking

Modelling is an effective way of supporting students' development as reflective thinkers. Teachers can model aspects of reflection such as:
- accessing prior knowledge — 'What do I already know about ...'
- linking new learning to what is already known — 'This reminds me of ...'

- synthesising information — 'This bit of information links to ...'
- self-evaluating — 'I was able to use ... to work out ...'

Providing Set Formats

Sometimes the teacher may wish to support the use of Learning Logs by having students record their reflections in a set way or think about one particular aspect of their learning.

Joint Construction

Jointly constructing Class Learning Logs provides further support by demonstrating the strategies used to reflect and the way a written log entry is constructed.

Class Learning Logs can be revisited many times to:
- enable students to reflect on what has been learnt over a period of time
- provide a model for students' own Learning Logs
- refresh students' memories about strategies they can use
- assist in the construction of Learning Journeys.

(Adapted from Wilson, J. and Wing Jan, L. 1993.)

Guiding Questions or Prompts for Learning Logs

Successes	Problems
• What worked well?	• What problems did you have?
• What did you enjoy?	

Changes
- What changes would you make if you used this strategy again?
- What changes would you make if you did this lesson again?

Puzzles
- What didn't you understand?
- What questions do you have for the teacher?

Sharing

I shared this reflection with _____

because _____

They suggested _____.

Figure 9.13: Adapted from Bennett, B., Rolheiser, C. and Stevahn, L. 1991.

11 Look What I Can Do

The 'Look What I Can Do' pages for each phase of the *First Steps* Maps of Development provide another framework to support students as they reflect on and represent their learning. The 'Look What I Can Do' statements are reflective of the Indicators in each phase of development. Indicators have been reworded into student-friendly terms. Students can rate themselves against the given statements. Once ratings have been completed, the statements can be used as a basis for setting future goals.

12 T-Charts

T-Charts require students to brainstorm and record information around two dimensions: 'What it looks like' and 'What it sounds like'. Students can reflect on the two statements individually and then share their information in small groups or with the whole class if desired.

Figure 9.14 is an example completed by a Year 4 class (eight– to nine–year-olds) after reflecting on a group discussion. Students were asked to think about what would be evident to an outsider observing effective groups in operation. The T-Chart forms the framework for goal-setting and is a way of improving future group work. It can be amended as needed.

Effective Group Work	
Looks like	**Sounds like**
• One person talking, the rest listening	• 'That's a good idea.'
• People looking at the speaker	• 'Could you repeat that? I'm not sure I understand.'
• Everyone on task	• 'What's your idea?'
• Looking interested	• 'Can you tell us a bit more about that?'
• Everyone having a chance to speak	• 'Can I add to that point?'

Figure 9.14: Effective group work — T-Chart

13 Y-Charts

Y-Charts are an extension of T-Charts. They include the two dimensions from T-Charts with the addition of a third: 'What does it feel like?'. Y-Charts are constructed in the same manner as T-Charts and can easily be adapted to use with many different processes or strategies.

Have-a-Go

Looks like ...
- trying different ways of writing a word
- checking the charts in the room

Sounds like ...
- 'I'm not sure which letter pattern to choose so I'll try **ee** and **ea** and see which one looks right.'
- 'Which way looks right?'

Feels like ...
- 'Wow, I can work this out.'
- 'I can do this.'

Figure 9.15: 'Have–a–Go' process — Y-Chart

14 KWHL Framework

A KWHL Framework can be used to represent the connection between what is already known and what is new. It can be used as a plan of action before learning begins and, later, to reflect and represent what was done.

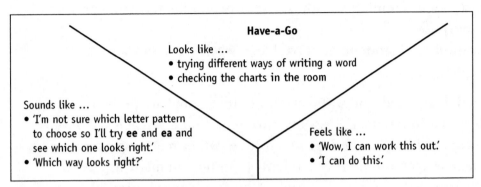

Know	Want	How	Learn
What do I know? •Dinosaurs ate meat and plants •Dinosaurs were different sizes •Dinosaurs lived long ago.	**What do I want to find out?** •What was the biggest dinosaur? •Why did dinosaurs die out? •Where did dinosaurs live?	**How can I find out what I want to learn?** •Check the library catalogues. •Do a Google search or the Internet. •Email the museum.	**What did I learn?**

Students complete this section at the conclusion of the topic or unit.

What should I do first?
Email the museum – it might take a while to get the answer.
Next I will book a space on the library computer to do a net search.
Then I will check the catalogues.

What I did well. What was successful?

Students complete this section at the conclusion of the topic or unit.

Figure 9.16: KWHL Framework

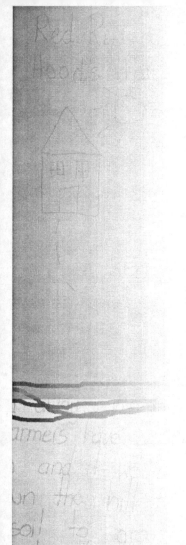

Ways of Reporting Learning

There are many different ways in which students can be encouraged to report on their learning. The type of reporting activity will depend on:

- the time available
- the time span; e.g. a single lesson or a whole unit of work
- the students' familiarity with the activity and the reporting process
- the purpose
- the number of students involved; e.g. whole class, small group, partners.

The activities listed under 'Five-minute Reporting' are probably more suited to reporting sessions during or after a single lesson. They are brief but can be highly effective. Other reporting activities may take longer and involve students reporting on many aspects of their learning. These may be used at the end of a unit of work.

1 'Five-minute Reporting'
2 Conferences
3 Jigsaw
4 Envoy
5 Inside/Outside Circles
6 Learning Journeys

1 'Five-minute Reporting'

- Have students turn to a partner and discuss some aspect of the lesson or strategies they have used. Ensure that both students have equal time as speaker and listener.
- Ask for volunteers to report their learning to the class. Ensure the students listening have the opportunity to question those reporting.
- Adhesive Notes: Students working individually or in pairs write one idea from their reflection on a note. Invite students to bring their notes and place them on a chart, board or flip-chart. Randomly select one or two notes from the board and have those students elaborate on their notes.

2 Conferences

Conferencing is purposeful talking and listening and is an excellent forum for reporting reflections and sharing representations of learning. Conferencing can occur in a variety of ways from one-on-one interactions between teacher and student to small-group peer conferencing. The conference can be used to reflect on literacy areas such as writing or on the strategies and processes of learning.

3 Jigsaw

Jigsaw promotes sharing and reporting of understandings or ideas. The strength of Jigsaw is that it promotes engagement and focus of individuals as each person is responsible for contributing to the sharing process.

- Form 'home groups' of three or four students. Allocate different tasks to each group. For example, read different chapters in a novel, find different letter patterns, or research different information about an animal. These home groups will become 'experts' in one particular area.

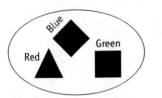 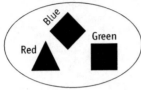 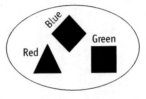

Figure 9.17: Home groups

- One member from each home group moves out to form a new group. This can be done by allocating a different number, colour or letter to the members of each home group. Similar numbers, colours or letters then get together to form new groups.

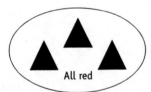 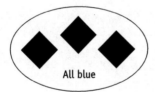 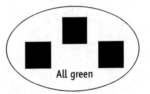

Figure 9.18: New groups

- Each member reports information from the home group task. Other members of the group listen and can question or record information.

4 Envoy

The Envoy strategy also promotes sharing or reporting of understandings and ideas.

- Allocate topics to home groups. Groups then discuss the topic and become the 'experts'.

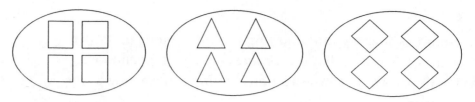

Figure 9.19: Home groups

- Allocate one person in the home group to be the spokesperson or envoy. The envoy moves to another group to report information about their topic.

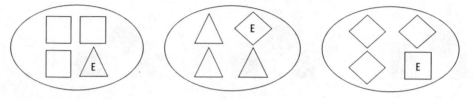

Figure 9.20: Envoys move to another group.

- After sharing information with the 'host group', the envoy becomes a listener. The host group shares their information.
- The envoy returns to their home group and shares what they have learnt from the host group.

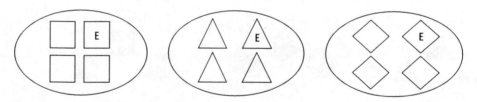

Figure 9.21: Envoys return to the home group.

5 Inside/Outside Circles

Inside/Outside Circles allow students to work in pairs to report information. (Kagan, S. 1990)

- Divide students into two groups. One group makes an inner circle and the other group forms a circle around this group.
- Students in the inner circle and the outer circle face each other to form pairs.
- Students take turns to report their information to their partner.
- At the end of a set period of time students are asked to move (e.g. **inner circle moves two places to the right**), creating new partners.
- Students now share their information with a new partner.

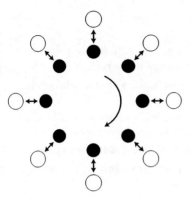

Figure 9.22: Inside/Outside Circles

6 Learning Journeys

Learning Journeys are a way for students to report learning to others. On a Learning Journey students physically take someone (parent, caregiver, sibling, relative) on a journey around the classroom to share their learning products and processes. Journeys provide an opportunity to report not only on what they have learnt but also on the way it was learnt. (Brockhoff, V. 1995)

Properly executed, a Learning Journey is more than a 'show and tell' of work sample books. It promotes metacognitive thinking as students prepare to share their learning with others. Learning Journeys provide opportunities for students to:

- report or demonstrate activities in the classroom; e.g. Shared Writing
- demonstrate procedures of games; e.g. Barrier Games
- discuss items and activities found in learning centres or special areas; e.g. science table
- point out and demonstrate how to use environmental print; e.g. Cumulative Charts
- discuss and demonstrate how independent work areas are used; e.g. the writing table, reading corner.

Planning a Learning Journey

- Students record major learnings from a given period of time; e.g. 'During last term, I learnt that the globe will only light up if a circuit is closed'. A maximum of five or six is appropriate.
- Students then consider activities or aspects of the classroom environment that will help them demonstrate their learning to others; e.g. technology table to demonstrate closed circuit. There should be at least one activity or demonstration for each major learning.
- Students plan, draw and write their Learning Journey, considering where and what they will share to illustrate their learning.

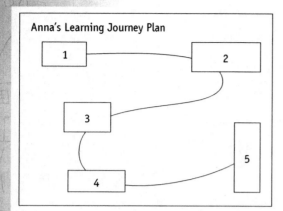

Anna's Learning Journey Plan

1 Science Table – I learnt that shells have different patterns. Explain why. Look through microscope to see patterns.
2 Computer Corner – I learnt how to insert video clips with music. Run PowerPoint presentation.
3 Technology Table – I learnt that to make the globe light up you have to have a closed circuit. I will show how to make it.
4 Library Corner – show favourite book and read favourite page.
5 Mathematics Centre – I learnt which shapes tessellate. Show how to make a pattern that tessellates.

Figure 9.23: A student's Learning Journey plan

- Rehearse the plan by taking another student on the journey. Encourage students to ask questions such as 'Why did you like this activity?', 'Was there anything that was challenging about this?', 'What would you do next time?'. Students make modifications to their Learning Journey if needed.
- Various supports such as guiding questions or checklists may be appropriate for students, depending on their age and experience.

Checklist for _____'s Learning Journey

- Introduce your visitor/s to your teacher.
- Take your visitor/s on a tour of the room, stopping at your selected places.
- Share your work or demonstrate the activity.
- Discuss your goals for next term/semester.
- Thank your visitor/s for coming.

Figure 9.24

Points for Teachers to Consider

- Inform visiting participants of what to expect from the Learning Journey and their role. Perhaps give some directions for asking questions and providing specific feedback. Teachers may also like to explain why Learning Journeys have been instigated. This process will need to be started well before the Learning Journeys are planned to allow for questions or concerns to be addressed.
- Organise a time for the Learning Journeys. Consider the availability of parents and caregivers when organising times. Before-school or after-school appointments may need to be made if many parents and caregivers work. Plans for the accommodation of younger siblings may also need to be considered.

- Timetable the Learning Journeys for the class so everyone doesn't arrive at the same time.
- Ensure that every student has someone to take on the Learning Journey. If parents are not available consider other relatives, older siblings or another teacher.
- After the Learning Journey the teacher, students and parents can reflect on the process and outcomes. This will help set directions or guidelines for future journeys.

Learning Journey Reflection Sheet

Student's Name _____

Date of Learning Journey _____

What was the best part? _____

_____

_____

What didn't work well? _____

_____

Suggestions _____

_____

_____

Figure 9.25

CHAPTER 10
Communicating with Parents

Developing Home–School Partnerships

This chapter has been written using the word 'parents' with the understanding that this term encompasses all adults who are responsible for the care and welfare of a child in the home.

Developing a strong home–school partnership is vital. Parental involvement is an integral part of all aspects of students' learning. In particular, parents play a pivotal role in supporting their child's literacy learning and are a rich source of information about their own child's literacy development.

This chapter looks at the ways in which teachers and schools can support and communicate with parents to maximise home–school partnerships. It offers general suggestions that could apply to any learning area. The *First Steps* Maps of Development in each strand offer further suggestions for helping parents to support literacy development in the home. A range of phase-specific activities are outlined in each phase and detailed further on the supporting CD-ROM.

Home–school communication generally falls into three broad categories:
• Raising Awareness
• Sharing Information
• Involving Parents.

Raising Awareness

Awareness-raising communication is designed to help parents understand the practices, procedures and function of the school. This is often achieved using informal conversations, announcements about the school's activities, weekly school newsletters or bulletins, open days, invitations to school functions and activities, school information booklets for new enrolments, and questionnaires. These types of communication are designed to establish rapport with parents and to give them a sense of confidence in the school. They encourage parents to feel more comfortable about contacting the school with regard to their children.

Sharing Information

Sharing information keeps parents informed about the policies, procedures, aims and expectations that exist in the school but more specifically in the classrooms. Communication of this type is generally between the classroom teacher and the parents and may be individualised and more formal in nature. Communication methods may include parent–teacher meetings, home visits, letters and notes, class newsletters, teacher–parent noticeboards, reports, phone and email correspondence, portfolios or work-sample packages and communication books. Parents can also be encouraged to share information about their child with the school or teacher. This helps to make the information sharing a two-way process.

Involving Parents

One goal of communication is to actively involve parents in the school and classroom. School-level involvement may include tasks such as helping out in the library or canteen, assisting with clerical work such as typing or coaching a sporting team. In-class involvement can take many forms including assisting during classroom activities at an instructional or support level, providing teacher-assistance by helping with displays, making games and activities, providing support during class outings and offering expertise for in-school events. For those parents who cannot be involved directly in the classroom, opportunities exist for them to provide support to the classroom programs through the work they do with their child at home; e.g. helping with home reading or research.

The Importance of Developing Partnerships with Parents

It is important that parents are:
- invited to provide information about their child's literacy development
- informed about their child's literacy development
- provided with information and strategies to support their child's literacy development in the home.

It is important for teachers to communicate with parents so that:
- parents have a better understanding of how teachers are helping students to achieve success at school
- parents learn how their children are progressing in their schooling
- parents learn ways they can support their children's learning at home

- parents understand that they have a role in influencing the priorities and practices of the school
- teachers have a better understanding of their students' background and experiences
- students see that the adults in their life care about them and are interested in their learning, family practices and home communities.

Raising Awareness and Sharing Information

Schools, teachers and parents have a mutual interest in promoting a student's learning. It is important to develop effective ways of raising awareness and sharing information, both written and oral*. Schools and teachers often experiment with a range of ways of communicating with parents until they discover those that are the most efficient for their situation and the ones they are most comfortable in using.

A variety of ways of communicating with parents are outlined in this section. These can be used either at the school level to raise awareness, or at the classroom level to share information. It is not practical or recommended that they all be implemented at one time.

1 Meet-the-teacher Night
2 Communication Books
3 Newsletters
4 Emails
5 Web Page
6 Faxes
7 Telephone
8 Informal Talks
9 Quick Notes
10 Conferences
11 Three-way Conferences
12 Bulletin Boards
13 Master or Monthly Calendar of Events
14 Report Cards, Portfolios, Work Samples
15 Surveys

*If English is another language for parents, it is advantageous to have written communications translated into the language used at home. This is not always easy but is worth pursuing. There are supports available within the community to enable this to happen.

1 Meet-the-teacher Night

This may be the first formal contact between the teacher and parents. These nights provide an opportunity for the teacher and aspects of the curriculum to be introduced. Possible topics during this session are:

- the teacher — parents will be interested to find out about the teacher as a person and about their relevant professional experiences and philosophies
- the classroom — discuss school and classroom policies and procedures, the curriculum, homework criteria, goals and expectations for students and instructional materials that will be used
- working together — outline how home and school can work together, inform parents about how, where and when the teacher can be contacted and discuss how parents can best support their child's learning.

A parent information booklet, which can be referred to during the year, may be provided at this time. This can provide parents with the language of the classroom and enable them to discuss school in terms that are familiar to their children.

2 Communication Books

Communication books have been used successfully as a form of two-way sharing between the home and the classroom. Each student has a personal communication book that allows the teacher and parents to share comments. These may be in praise of a particular achievement, related to an area of focus, or general comments about the student. Parents should be encouraged to exchange comments with the teacher, providing information about literacy development in the home.

3 Newsletters

Newsletters sent home can inform parents about aspects of the classroom. These may include reminders about upcoming events, samples of students' work, topics of study or ideas for support at home.

If it is not practicable to produce a class newsletter, teachers can ensure something from their classroom is reported in the regular whole-school newsletter.

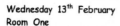

Wednesday 13th February
Room One

Dear Parents
Thank you for your support with:
- punctuality – most children are arriving by 8.30am – and this has meant a smooth start to the day.
- ensuring your child is given the responsibility of unpacking their bags and coming into the room by themselves. They are coping very well.
- sharing their home reader with them and filling in the Reading Record sheet.
- having their name on EVERYTHING !

Each child needs a large shirt for Art. Please make sure it is easy to fasten and the sleeves are an appropriate length.

The Year Two teachers have decided not to give extra Homework this term. We would like the children to continue Home Reading each week night. We thought, with the very hot weather and the 'break' from usual lessons because of swimming lessons and the Easter holidays later in the term, that it would be better to wait until Term Two before sending home 'other' Homework.

**** Our class is beginning a theme of work about _Transport._ As part of this program we are going to design and construct 'vehicles' that move. Therefore we need HUNDREDS of boxes and the rolls from plastic/foil wraps. Boxes no bigger than cereal packets or shoe-boxes would be very helpful. ****

If anyone is able to get off-cuts of card or paper that I could use for charts/flashcards I would really appreciate it.

I am very pleased with the way the children are settling into the new year:
- Basic routines are being established.
- They are beginning to operate in small groups where they are not being directly supervised.
- Work habits such as concentrating on the task, persevering before asking for assistance, effort to improve neatness etc are developing.

Perhaps the only area that needs some attention, with quite a number of the children, is correct pencil grip.

If you wish to see me to discuss any aspect of the program and/or if there is any information you think would be beneficial for me to know, in order to better help your child – please see me to organise a mutually convenient time for us to meet.

Thanks again for your support.
Regards
Jill Van Dyl.

Figure 10.1: Sample class newsletter

4 Emails

Email addresses of parents can be used to send information quickly. Students without an email address can receive a printout of the email sent home. Email also allows quick responses from the parents if the need arises.

5 Web Page

Some schools or individual teachers create a website that parents can visit to find out what is happening in the classroom. It is worthwhile giving parents access to information on current events, assignments, current and future projects, as well as any necessary reminders.

Figure 10.2: Sample school website

6 Faxes

Some parents may prefer communication via a fax rather than email or a website page. Sending faxes is another option to keep parents informed and involved.

Note: Students can be involved in the creation of any of the above messages. These are ideal opportunities to model and discuss purpose, audience, context and forms of writing.

7 Telephone

Teachers often make contact with parents when things go wrong, so why not call when they go right? Make positive phone calls. Let parents know that their child has done something worthy of a phone call — they have achieved a goal that has been set, passed an assessment task or completed a great presentation.

8 Informal Talks

Teachers often make use of informal opportunities to share information with parents; e.g. before and after school.

9 Quick Notes

Let parents know that their child has done something 'good' through written communication in the form of letters, informal notes or certificates. These are often well received and keep parents informed about what is happening in the classroom.

An Apple from the Teacher

15 March

Dear Mrs Johnston

Just wanted to let you know that Andrea did a terrific job presenting her report on 'Teeth'. Her PowerPoint presentation was informative and entertaining. She spoke expressively and the picture slides she included really added to the presentation. I hope you are as proud of the work she is doing as she is!

Sincerely

Sue Lynch

Figure 10.3: A teacher-to-parent note

Sunnymount School

is our
STUDENT OF THE WEEK
because

Congratulations

Figure 10.4

10 Conferences

Conferences allow parents and teachers to meet face-to-face. This is valuable because most people can express themselves more completely and openly in person*. The opportunity to ask follow-up questions or elaborate on specific points in face-to-face meetings allows any misunderstandings or misconceptions to be clarified.

*For parents with limited English it may be necessary to organise translators for these conferences. Translators may be a relative, a friend, another teacher or someone from an outside agency.

Conferences should be held at a time when parents can meet and plan with the teacher to ensure their child's success in school. Well-conducted parent–teacher conferences can accomplish several goals.

- Teachers learn first-hand about the child's home-learning environment.
- Parents find out how their child is progressing academically, socially, and emotionally.
- Parents and teachers can celebrate successes and discuss areas for further or future development. Teachers can share information based on *First Steps* Maps of Development if they wish.
- Parents can ask about any aspects of the curriculum and classroom policies; e.g. **homework, discipline, attendance.**
- Teachers and parents can develop a mutual action plan to help ensure the child's success in school.

Teachers may wish to make notes before the conference so that important information is not forgotten. A suggested plan may include any or all of the following:

- Begin on a positive note by remarking on unique qualities of the student.
- Discuss the student's strengths and weaknesses.
- Share and discuss academic and social goals for the rest of the year (if appropriate). Discuss any issues related to these goals.
- Ask for parent input on the student's current performance and social development.

---

11 Three-way Conferences

Three-way conferences allow the teacher, parent and student all to have input into a discussion about the student's development over time. They provide an ideal opportunity for reporting and sharing information with parents. These conferences can be led by the student and may incorporate a 'journey' around the classroom, pre-conference observation of the student in the classroom and/or the sharing of a portfolio collection.

Before the Conference

- Prepare students for the conference. This includes teaching them how to collect evidence of their learning, how to review their goals, how to create personal action plans and how to share their reflections about learning; e.g. **'To learn about … I had to …'**
- Prepare parents for the conference by providing them with background information outlining the procedure to be followed and their role in it.

During the Conference

- The student shares a collection of work samples.
- The student leads the discussion on what has been learnt, what areas need to be worked on and the goals that have been chosen for the next teaching and learning period.
- Learning goals proposed by the student are discussed, modified if necessary and agreed on.
- The student discusses their plan of action to achieve these goals, and the teacher and parent agree to provide the necessary support.
- The teacher ensures that the conference runs smoothly by helping the student address the issues and answering questions that arise.

After the Conference

- The teacher records the discussion from the conference and any specific information about goals, support or follow-up that may be needed.

12 Bulletin Boards

Bulletin boards outside the classroom door can be used to communicate with parents about numerous things; e.g. **upcoming events, class and student achievements, rosters for classroom volunteers.** A copy of any vital information posted on the bulletin board will need to be sent home to parents who may not view the board. Whenever possible involve students in contributing to and maintaining the bulletin board.

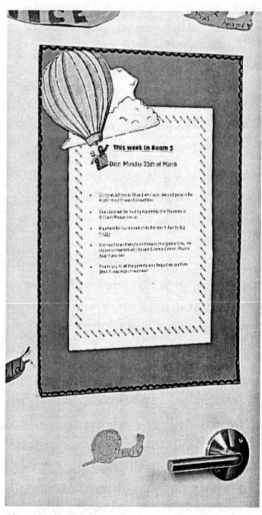

Class bulletin board

13 Master or Monthly Calendar of Events

A calendar that outlines events for a given period can be sent home to parents. At the beginning of the year this could be a general outline of the events that are known at that time. Then a monthly update providing more detail could be sent.

WESTERN PRIMARY SCHOOL

TERM 4

WEEK	MONDAY	TUESDAY	WEDNESDAY	THURSDAY	FRIDAY
1	October 14	October 15	October 16	October 17	October 18
			Year 7 camp	Close 2.30pm	
2	October 21	October 22	October 23 Education Week Breakfast	October 24 Assembly Yr 5	October 25 PHOTOS wear uniform
				Close 2.30pm	Portfolios go home
3	October 28	October 29 School Nurse Visiting	October 30 SCHOOL REVIEW VISIT	October 31 Assembly Yr 2	November 1
				Close 2.30pm	
4	November 4	November 5	November 6 S W I M M I N G	November 7	November 8
			Donna Smith Science visit $4 1.45	Assembly Yr 6 Close 2.30pm	
5	November 11	November 12	November 13 S W I M M I N G	November 14	November 15
				New phone installation	Transition Day 1.15 Yr 7 to DSHS
	P&C Meeting			Close 2.30pm	P&C Car Boot sale SATURDAY
6	November 18	November 19 Fitness/skills assessment Yrs 1-7	November 20 Fitness/skills assessment Yrs 1-7	November 21 Assembly Yr 3	November 22
	MIS Data Collection Week		COUNCIL MEETING 3.10	Close 2.30pm	
7	November 25 2003 Kindy Parents meeting at Kindy 9.00am	November 26	November 27	November 28	November 29 School Professional Development Day *STUDENTS DO NOT ATTEND*
				Close 2.30pm	
8	December 2 Parent/Teacher/ Student interview week	December 3 Choir Performance at Shopping Centre	December 4	December 5	December 6
				Close 2.30pm	
9	December 9 Reports go home	December 10 School Nurse Visiting	December 11	December 12 P&C Christmas Stall Thank you morning tea for parents (Staff/students)	December 13 P&C Christmas Stall
	P&C Meeting		Staff meeting 3.20pm	Close 2.30pm	
10	December 16	December 17	December 18 PRESENTATION NIGHT	December 19 STUDENTS' LAST DAY School Disco	December 20

Figure 10.5

14 Report Cards, Portfolios, Work Samples

Sending home samples of students' work on a regular basis is an excellent way of communicating with parents about student progress. Although portfolios and formal report cards are often sent home at predetermined dates, work samples can be sent as teachers judge it appropriate or in line with school policy.

15 Surveys

It is beneficial if communication occurs both ways between the home and school. Parents know a lot about their children and this information can provide teachers with valuable insights into classroom behaviour and academic achievement. Sending home surveys for parents to complete is an excellent way of finding out more about students in a classroom.

ROOM 4's READING SURVEY

Your input would be greatly valued to help me understand your child's strengths and needs in reading. Please complete the form and return it to school by Friday 25th.

Student's name: _____

1. Are any languages other than English spoken at home? If yes, please list them. _____
   _____

2. Ways I currently help my child with reading are: _____
   _____
   _____
   _____

3. When reading, my child particularly enjoys:
   _____
   _____
   _____
   _____

4. In relation to reading, my child's special strengths are: _____
   _____
   _____
   _____

5. When reading, my child has difficulty with:
   _____
   _____
   _____
   _____

6. My child's special interests outside school are: _____
   _____
   _____

7. I would like more information about: _____
   _____
   _____
   _____

Thank you for your time.

Figure 10.6: Adapted from Rhodes, L. and Shanklin, N. 1993

Involving Parents

There are various ways in which parents can support their child's education both at the school and classroom level. Some parents may be able to assist within the classroom on a regular basis while others, due to other commitments, may help outside of school hours on an intermittent basis.

It's a good idea to send home surveys or questionnaires regularly. These may provide a list of ways in which parents can be involved in the school or classroom. By inviting parents to be involved, teachers are acknowledging the valuable contribution and expertise that parents can offer to the school or class.

Parents can:
- volunteer to help in the classroom for a given period of time or during a particular lesson; e.g. read to students, help during writing, science or art
- assist on field trips and excursions
- be a guest speaker and address the class on an area of expertise, about an interest or an experience; e.g. a chef could demonstrate cooking
- perform tasks outside the classroom; e.g. covering books, making resource materials
- provide resources for a particular topic; e.g. photographs taken on a trip
- join the school parent or community group
- participate in any cultural or historical events that the school or class celebrates.

Mount Bulla Parent Survey

Name: _____

Child's name: _____

When are you able to volunteer? Circle your choice.
- morning
- afternoon
- evening
- weekly
- monthly
- occasionally

What day suits you best? _____

How can you help?

☐ assist in the classroom

☐ guest speaker — topic? _____

☐ clerical (publishing materials etc.)

☐ tutor/mentor — ☐ Literacy ☐ Numeracy

☐ library assistance

☐ assist with excursions or field trips

☐ translate materials

☐ other

Figure 10.7: Sample parent survey adapted from Power, B. 1999

Helping Parents Support Literacy Development

Parents often request help in supporting their children's literacy development. In this section there are suggestions about how the teacher can assist parents to help their children. Teachers can make selections that are most appropriate to their context and to the particular parent group.

1 Open-door Policy
2 Parent Workshops
3 Family Nights
4 Activities from the CD-ROM
5 Guest Speakers
6 Videos of Good Practice
7 Literacy Articles
8 Recommended Reading Lists, Websites
9 Information Brochures, Fridge Cards

1 Open-door Policy

Let parents know that during certain times of the week the classroom door is open and they are welcome to come in and watch students work. Encourage parents to give advance notice of a visit to avoid timetable clashes with activities such as excursions and sport. Make it clear that during these visits the focus will be on parents observing the class so they will understand more about their child's learning. This time is not an opportunity to discuss a student's progress with the teacher. The teacher's responsibility at this time is to the students, not the parent. Teachers might distribute a handout that lists things the parents could observe; e.g. 'Notice how the students use prediction during this lesson.'

This Shared Reading lesson involves prediction.

Here are some key points to note as you observe this lesson.
- Notice how the children are encouraged to think about the meaning of the story, using the title and illustrations, before reading.
- Note how the children are encouraged to read the predictable parts of the book.
- Observe the way the teacher points to the print to reinforce that words convey meaning.
- Notice the importance of the illustrations in helping children understand the book.
- Notice what questions are asked about the book.

Adapted from Cairney, T. and Munsie, L. 1992

2 Parent Workshops

Plan workshops so parents can learn about and try out activities that students are experiencing. This allows parents to feel more confident and more able to assist their children at home. These workshops also provide an opportunity for the teacher to explain why particular methodologies such as the use of investigation, modelled writing, guided reading or project work are used in the classroom.

3 Family Nights

Family nights focusing on a particular learning area allow parents to work with their children and be involved in activities that are used in the classroom, e.g. maths or science night, music or art activities.

4 Activities from the CD-ROM

In the phases of the *First Steps* Map of Development Books there is a suggested list of activities that parents can do at home to support their child. The CD-ROM for each strand provides more detailed explanations of these activities. Teachers can select appropriate activities to be copied and sent home for parents to use.

5 Guest Speakers

Organising guest speakers to address parents on selected topics can be very beneficial; e.g. children's author or child-safety councillor.

6 Videos of Good Practice

Videos or CD-ROMs that support parents' understanding of literacy development can be made available for borrowing. The flexibility in the use of these videos can be appealing to busy parents.

7 Literacy Articles

It may be beneficial for teachers to collect education or literacy articles on topics that provide useful information for parents. These may come from a variety of sources such as professional books, journal articles, weekly magazines or the local newspaper. Have these available for parents to access. Selected extracts or articles may be sent home to all parents.

8 Recommended Reading Lists, Websites

Keep parents informed about places to find recommended reading lists for their children and websites that provide useful educational information. Direct them to the Children's Book Council, local bookshops and newspapers that often have this type of information readily available. Websites such as *National Geographic* or *The Discovery Channel* have sections for children. Many children's authors have now developed their own websites which are often worth a visit. Child-friendly search engines can also prove to be invaluable.

9 Information Brochures, Fridge Cards

Teacher-created or commercially produced brochures and cards can provide information about a particular literacy idea or offer suggestions about ways parents can support development at home.

How to Support Your Child as a Reader

- Read with and to your child every
  day and talk about the
  - information
  - pictures
  - story
  - message.

- It helps if you find books your
  child likes.

- If the book is ...
  - hard — you read it
  - easy — your child reads it
  - just right — take turns.

READ, READ, READ!
Reading skills develop through reading.

**Figure 10.8: Adapted
from ALEA Fridge Cards**

The staff of Universal School developed a brochure to be sent home to parents to inform them about *First Steps*. The staff included the benefits of *First Steps*, what it would look like in the classrooms and one simple idea parents could try at home.

First Steps Writing

Universal School   September

Information for Parents

First Steps is a professional development program which helps teachers support students in writing. Instruction is geared to teaching students to write clearly and concisely, using correct spelling, punctuation and grammar, while keeping their audience and purpose in mind.

For example, many third grade students are in the Early Writing Phase. Early Writers are able to write simple sentences but may have difficulty putting sentences together in paragraphs. A teaching suggestion is to introduce a number of sentences about a science or social studies topic that has been studied. Students work in groups to compose a paragraph using the sentences, being careful to add details to the topic sentence.

Why *First Steps*?

One of the goals of the district Language Arts Committee is to renew the focus on reading and writing in our schools. The committee reviewed the *First Steps* Writing resource and concluded that it would assist teachers in optimising student achievement in writing. *First Steps* provides teachers with tools to use in assessing and helping students to progress in writing.

Figure 10.9: Sample brochure for parents

First Steps is founded on a belief that effective teachers and schools share the responsibility of implementing a cohesive learning program and have high expectations for their students. As a partner in education, parents have a significant role to play in any school.

Parents need to be welcomed into schools and classrooms and kept informed about what is happening in education. Routman (1991) suggests that when teachers and schools:
- create opportunities for parents to see themselves as a vital, continuing part of their child's education, and
- develop open lines of communication that build trust,

parents are in a better position to support the learning process at home and demonstrate support of the school in the wider community.

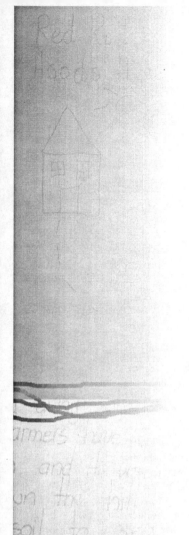

Glossary

analysing
a teaching and learning practice involving examination of the parts to understand the whole

applying
a teaching and learning practice involving the independent use of a skill, strategy or understanding to achieve a purpose

assessment
gathering data about students

Assisted Reading
a practice that involves a student reading in tandem with an accomplished reader

Authors Circle
a procedure involving students sharing a text they have written in a small group; members take turns to give the author positive feedback and suggestions for improvement

automaticity
bringing information to mind with little or no effort because a skill or understanding is so well known; e.g. the fast, accurate recognition of single words when reading

Book Discussion Group
a small group of students who meet to discuss a text they have chosen to read

code-switching
changing from one language to another during spoken or written communication so the finished text contains elements of both languages

context
the broad linguistic, social and cultural experiences that are brought to a situation

Contextual Understanding
understanding how the context affects the creation and interrelation of a text and the choice of language and images

Conventions
the structures and features of texts; e.g. spelling, grammar, pronunciation, text layout

critical literacy
the analysis and questioning of texts to reveal the values and beliefs that attempt to position the users

discussing
a teaching and learning practice involving the exchange of opinions on topics, themes or issues

EAD
English as an Additional Dialect — includes forms of non-standard English

EAL
English as an Additional Language — alternative term for ESL

evaluation
when judgements are made about students from data gathered

familiarising
a teaching and learning practice involving raising awareness and activating prior knowledge

fish bowl
a modelling technique that involves students seated around the perimeter of the room observing two or three groups of students rehearsing a process

flexible grouping
groups formed and dissolved depending on the goal of a lesson

formative evaluation
judgements made about a learner or the learning program as it progresses towards its final goals, aims or objectives

Global Statement	a written snapshot of a learner in a particular phase of development which encapsulates the typical characteristics of that phase
graphic organisers	visual representations of concepts that enable a learner to visualise, record and retrieve information from a text
Guided Reading	a procedure where teachers guide small groups of students as they read a common text assigned by the teacher with the aim of teaching and practising reading strategies
Guided Speaking and Listening	a procedure where teachers guide small groups of students as they construct spoken texts with the aim of teaching and practising oral strategies
Guided Viewing	a procedure where teachers guide small groups of students as they view a common text with the aim of teaching and practising viewing strategies
Guided Writing	a procedure where teachers guide the construction of a text with the aim of teaching and practising writing strategies
guiding	a teaching and learning practice involving the provision of scaffolding through strategic assistance at predetermined checkpoints in the learning process
indicator	a description of a literacy behaviour
innovating	a teaching and learning practice involving the alteration or amendment of a text to create a new one
investigating	a teaching and learning practice that involves finding, analysing, questioning and using information for a purpose
Key Indicator	a description of literacy behaviours that most students display at a phase of development
Language Experience	a procedure based on the idea that an experience can be shared, talked about, written down and then read about and re-read
Learning Journey	a way of reporting learning to others that involves students discussing and demonstrating what has been learnt and the way it was learnt
literacy	the ability to read, write, speak, listen, and view, to achieve a variety of purposes for oneself or a range of audiences
Major Teaching Emphases	teaching priorities appropriate to phases of development
metacognition	thinking about one's thinking
Modelled Reading	a reading procedure typified by the teacher selecting and reading a text to students and thinking aloud about the strategies that are being used
Modelled Speaking and Listening	a speaking and listening procedure typified by the teacher constructing a text for students and thinking aloud about the strategies that are being used
Modelled Viewing	a viewing procedure typified by the teacher viewing a text with students and thinking aloud about the strategies that are being used
Modelled Writing	a writing procedure where the teacher constructs a text for students and thinks aloud about the strategies being used

modelling	a teaching and learning practice involving explicitly thinking aloud to show how and why something is done
phase	a clustering of behaviours along a Map of Development
playing	a teaching and learning practice involving the exploration of concepts and skills through imagining and creating
practising	a teaching and learning practice involving the rehearsal of a skill or strategy
print-rich environment	an environment filled with meaningful print
Processes and Strategies	application of knowledge and understandings to comprehend and compose texts
pro forma	a prescribed format with sections to be filled in
Read and Retell	an activity described by Brown and Cambourne (1987) involving students in predicting, sharing, reading, writing, listening and justifying
Readers' Theatre	an oral reading of a script where the focus is on interpreting the text and creating the script rather than memorising it
reflecting	a teaching and learning practice involving thinking about the what, how and why of previous experiences
reporting	sharing learning with others
representing	demonstrating learning; eg. by drawing a picture, constructing a graphic organiser or writing key words
rubric	a recording framework featuring short descriptive statements along a continuum of excellence focusing on varied criteria
Shared Reading	an interactive reading procedure where students see the text, observe a good model (usually the teacher) reading it and are invited to read along
Shared Speaking and Listening	an interactive procedure where the teacher and students jointly construct an oral text
Shared Viewing	an interactive procedure where the teacher and students jointly construct meaning from a visual text; create a visual text
Shared Writing	an interactive procedure where students see the construction of a text by a good model (usually the teacher) and are invited to contribute ideas and suggestions; (the 'control of the pen' remains with the model)
sharing	a teaching and learning practice that involves the joint construction of meaning; e.g. between teacher and students, or student and student
simulating	a teaching and learning practice involving the adoption of a role or imagining oneself in a hypothetical setting
sociocultural	a combination of social and cultural factors such as economic status, geographical location, beliefs and values
strand	one of the four interwoven language mode; e.g. Reading, Writing, Speaking and Listening, Viewing

strategy	the mental processes used 'to do something you want to do'
substrand	one of the four interwoven lenses through which student performance in literacy can be monitored and supported; e.g. Use of Texts, Contextual Understanding, Conventions, Processes and Strategies
summative evaluation	the final judgements made to determine the degree to which goals, aims or objectives have been reached
targeted feedback	specific information given to direct, improve or control present and future learning
text	any communication from which meaning is gained; e.g. books, videos, Internet, website, conversation
text deconstruction	analysing a text section by section, to reveal its organisation, structure and language features
text reconstruction	putting a text together; e.g. from jumbled paragraphs
transforming	a teaching and learning practice involving the re-creation of a text or object in another genre, form, mode, medium or format; e.g. turning a story into a play, or a book into a film
use of texts	the composition and comprehension of texts

Bibliography

Anthony, R., Johnson, T., Mickleson, N. and Preece, A. 1991, *Evaluating Literacy*, Heinemann, Portsmouth, New Hampshire, USA.

Ashman, A. and Elkins, J. 2002, *Educating Children with Diverse Abilities*, Pearson Education, Australia.

Australian Literacy Educators' Association (ALEA) Fridge Cards.

Bailes, J. (ed.) 1980, *The Reading Bug and How to Catch It*, Ashton Scholastic, Sydney, Australia.

Beecher, B. and Arthur, L. 2001, *Play and Literacy in Children's Worlds*, Primary English Teaching Association (PETA), Newtown, New South Wales, Australia.

Bennett, B. 1995, Pen Note 102, Primary English Teaching Association (PETA), Newtown, New South Wales, Australia.

Bennett, B., Rolheiser, C. and Stevahn, L. 1991, *Cooperative Learning: Where Heart Meets Mind*, Educational Connections, Toronto, Ontario and Professional Development Associates, Bothell, Washington, USA.

Bennett, B. and Smilanich, P. 1994, *Classroom Management: A Thinking and Caring Approach*, Bookation Inc., Toronto, Ontario, Canada.

Berry, R. and Hudson, J. 1997, *Making the Jump: A Resource Book for Teachers of Aboriginal Students*, CEO, Kimberley District, Catholic Education Office, Western Australia.

Blakey, E. and Spence, S. 1990, *Developing Metacognition*, ERIC Digest, ERIC Clearinghouse on Information Resources, Syracuse, New York, USA.

Board of Studies 1995, *Curriculum and Standards Framework: English*, Carlton, Victoria, Australia.

Breen, M. *et al* 1997, *Profiling ESL Children*, Vol. 1: Key Issues and Findings, Department of Employment, Education, Training and Youth Affairs, Canberra, Australia.

Brockhoff, V. 1995, *Learning Journeys*, Practically Primary, Vol. 1, Australian Literacy Educators' Association (ALEA), Carlton, Victoria, Australia.

Brown, H. and Cambourne, B. 1987, *Read and Retell*, Heinemann, Portsmouth, New Hampshire, USA.

Cairney, T. and Munsie, L. 1992, *Beyond Tokenism — Parents as Partners in Literacy*, Australian Reading Association, Victoria, Australia.

Canter, L. and Canter, M. 1991, *Parents on Your Side*, Canter and Assoc., Santa Monica, California, USA.

Clarke, J., Wideman, R. and Eadie, S. 1990, *Together We Learn*, Prentice-Hall, Ontario, Canada.

Coughlin, D. 2000, *The Mainstreaming Handbook: How To Be an Advocate for Your Special Needs Students*, Heinemann, Portsmouth, New Hampshire, USA.

Curriculum Corporation 1994, *A Statement on English for Australian Schools*, Carlton, Victoria, Australia.

Davies, A., Cameron, C., Politano, C. and Gregory, K. 1994, *Together Is Better*, Eleanor Curtain Publishing, Armadale, Victoria, Australia.

Dekkers, S. 1996, *Voices in the Classroom*, Australian Literacy Educators' Association (ALEA) National Conference 1996, Adelaide, South Australia.

Education Department of Western Australia 1994, *Supporting Linguistic and Cultural Diversity Through First Steps: The Highgate Project*, Perth, Western Australia.

Education Department of Western Australia 1998, *English Student Outcome Statements*, Perth, Western Australia.

Evans, J. 1991, *Teachers Guide for Remote Schools*, Ministry of Education, Western Australia.

Freeman, Y. and Freeman, D. 1998, *ESL/EFL Teaching: Principles for Success*, Heinemann, Portsmouth, New Hampshire, USA.

Fullan, M. 1991, *The New Meaning of Educational Change*, Teachers College Press, Columbia University, New York, USA.

Fullan, M. 1993, *Change Forces*, The Falmer Press, Pennsylvania, USA.

Fullan, M. 1999, *Change Forces: The Sequel*, The Falmer Press, Pennsylvania, USA.

Fullan, M. 2001, *The New Meaning of Educational Change*, Third Edition, Irwin Publishing Ltd, Toronto, Ontario, Canada.

Garner, R. 1997, 'Metacognition and Self-Monitoring Strategies' in *What Research Has to Say About Reading*, Chapter 10, International Reading Association.

Guskey, T. R. 2000, *Evaluating Professional Development*, Corwin Press Inc., Thousand Oaks, California, USA.

Hammond, J. (ed.) 2001, *Scaffolding teaching and learning in language and literacy education*, Primary English Teaching Association (PETA), Newtown, New South Wales, Australia.

Hill, S. and Hill, T. 1990, *The Collaborative Classroom*, Eleanor Curtain Publishing, Armadale, Victoria, Australia.

Joyce, B. and Showers. B. 1995, *Student Achievement Through Staff Development*, Longman Publishers, White Plains, New York, USA.

Kagan, S. 1990, *Cooperative Learning: Resources for Teachers*, Resources for Teachers Inc., San Juan Capistrano, California, USA.

Kaufman, D. 2000, *Conferences and Conversations*, Heinemann, Portsmouth, New Hampshire, USA.

Kirkpatrick, D. L. 1996, 'Great Ideas Revisited. Techniques for evaluating training programs', *Training and Development Journal*, 50(1).

Kordalewski, J. 1999, *Incorporating Student Voice in Teaching Practice*, ERIC Digest, ERIC Clearinghouse on Teaching and Teacher Education, Washington DC, USA.

Kuhs, T., Johnson, R., Agruso, S. and Monrad, D. 2001, *Put to the Test*, Heinemann, Portsmouth, New Hampshire, USA.

Loucks-Horsley, S., Harding, C., Arbuckle, M., Murray, L., Dubea, C. and Williams, M. 1987, *Continuing to Learn: A Guidebook for Teacher Development*, The Regional Laboratory for Educational Improvement of the Northeast and Islands, Andover, Massachusetts, USA.

Loucks-Horsley, S., Hewson, P., Love, N. and Stiles, K. 1998, *Designing Professional Development for Teachers of Science and Mathematics*, Corwin Press Inc., Thousand Oaks, California, USA.

National Staff Development Council 2001, *Standards for Staff Development*, Oxford, Ohio, USA.

Nicoll, V. (ed.) 1996, *May I See Your Program Please?*, Primary English Teaching Association (PETA), New South Wales, Australia.

North Central Regional Education Laboratory, *High Expectations*, www.ncrel.org

Opitz, M. F. 1998, *Flexible Grouping in Reading*, Scholastic Professional Books, New York, USA.

Owocki, G. 1999, *Literacy Through Play*, Heinemann, Portsmouth, New Hampshire, USA.

Power, B. 1999, *Parent Power Energising Home–School Communication*, Heinemann, Portsmouth, New Hampshire, USA.

Rhodes, L. and Shanklin N. 1993, *Windows into Literacy: Assessing Learners K–8*, Heinemann, Portsmouth, New Hampshire, USA.

Rickards, D. and Cheek, E. 1999, *Designing Rubrics for K–6 Assessment*, Christopher Gordon Publications, Norwood, Massachusetts, USA.

Routman, R. 1991, *Invitations: Changing as Teachers and Learners K–12*, Heinemann, Portsmouth, New Hampshire, USA.

Routman, R. 2000, *Conversations: Strategies for Teaching, Learning and Evaluating*, Heinemann, Portsmouth, New Hampshire, USA.

Sandstrom, R. (ed.) 1994, *Programming for Literacy Learning*, Shortrun Books, Australia.

South Australia Department of Education, Training and Development 2000, *ESL in the Mainstream: Teacher Development Course*.

Strickland, K. and Strickland, J. 2000, *Making Assessment Elementary*, Heinemann, Portsmouth, New Hampshire, USA.

Vogt, L., Jordan, C. and Tharp, R. 1987, 'Explaining school failure, producing school success: two cases', *Anthropology and Education Quarterly*, 18.

Wilson, J. and Wing Jan, L. 1993, *Thinking for Themselves: Developing Strategies for Reflective Learning*, Eleanor Curtain Publishing, Armadale, Victoria, Australia.